LIFE STORY

A

PRIZE AUTOBIOGRAPHY

By JAMES I. HILLOCKS

AUTHOR OF

SOPHIA, A GLANCE AT SOCIETY.   VIOLA, THE PROVOST'S DAUGHTER.
AN HUMBLE OFFERING.   SUGGESTIVE READINGS.
THE NEW WRITER.   THOUGHTS IN RHYME,
ETC. ETC.

The tale of a human being has to every human being a very deep interest.---
Rev. Dr. JOHN R. BEARD.

LONDON: HOULSTON & WRIGHT, W. TWEEDIE.
EDINBURGH: J. MENZIES, W. OLIPHANT & Co.
DUBLIN: J. ROBERTSON.   MANCHESTER: W. BREMNER.
GLASGOW: THOMAS MURRAY & SON, W. LOVE, G. GALLIE.

TO

MAGGIE,

MY BELOVED AND LOVING WIFE,

THIS LITTLE BOOK IS

AFFECTIONATELY DEDICATED.

CONTENTS.

VI.

PREFACE.

EARLY in May, 1856, a worthy friend called my attention to the fact, that in February of that year, Twenty Prizes were offered for the best "Lives of Working Men, written by themselves;" and that Professor Blackie, Edinburgh; Professor Nichol, Glasgow; Patrick E. Dove, Esq., Edinburgh; and Peter Bayne, M.A., were the gentlemen who had consented to undertake the duties of adjudication. The manner and matter of the announcements to which my friend referred, and which appeared in the *Commonwealth*, as also the very mention of these names, coupled with that of the worthy proprietor of that respectable newspaper, were enough to induce one to think of doing his best as a competitor. The question, Am I eligible? presented itself to my mind; but a letter from the proper quarter soon informed me that it was such Autobiographies as I could send that were wanted. Another obstacle came in view. The papers had all to be forwarded to the office of the *Commonwealth*, on or before the 15th May, so that there were only nine or ten days left from which to snatch a few spare hours to make the necessary effort, and hence the question with me was, Could I, in that short space of time, do anything like justice to my subject? Yet I felt this difficulty was, in part, removed when my friend pointed out that

"The givers of the prizes left each competitor to his own taste and judgment. They only stipulated that the lives be *genuine, truthful narratives.*"

I came to the end of my story on the 14th. The title was "THE WEAVER'S SON," and the motto accompanying it, "*Onward and Upward.*" In the newspaper of the 17th I read :—

"Our offer of a number of Prizes for the best Autobiographies of Working Men has been vigorously responded to. *We have received nearly eighty Autobiographies.*"

Having fought, I wished to win. I was very uneasy during the unavoidable delay caused by the examination of such a great mass of MSS. At last twenty were selected—ten as first class, and ten as second class; and glad was I to learn, by letter from Mr. Rae, as well as by the announcement in the *Commonwealth*, that my name appeared among the *first class*, followed by the words "Formerly weaver, now teacher, Dundee." The adjudication was signed by J. P. Nichol, LL.D.; P. E. Dove, Esq.; and Peter Bayne, M.A. A foot-note stated that in consequence of protracted absence from home, Professor Blackie had not been able to act as an adjudicator.

So much for my friend's hint and its result. But that is not all. The donor of the prizes has since very kindly made me a present of my MS., and given me full liberty to make the best of it. For a time I was undecided as to whether or not this Autobiography should be published. Among other reasons for now offering it to the reading public, is the fact of its having taken the position it did among so many productions, concerning all of which these and many such expressions were given forth from time to time in the leaders of the *Commonwealth :—*

"We have looked carefully into the MSS. (the Autobiographies) before us, and are in a position to convey to the public the general impression we have formed of their contents. * * We doubt if there was ever before collected, in any shape, so large, so fresh, so varied, and so instructive a mass of information touching the condition of the working classes. * * They reflect, with accuracy and completeness, every circumstance of the lives of their authors and their class. * * The features of natures are broadly, distinctly and fairly given. * * It has been said that romance is around us if we could see it; that comedy still laughs at births and bridals, however dull it may be on the stage; and that tragedy, whether with sceptred pall or no, has still death-beds worthy of a Shakspeare's pen. The fact is strangely brought out in the pages before us. * * The gloss of the novel is rubbed off, but it is well supplied by the sterner lines of facts. * * Our endeavour to obtain a comprehensive and accurate exhibition of the life of the body of the people has been eminently successful."

Such were some of the leading ideas gathered from a careful reading of the whole MSS.; and I may here mention two of the special elements named as giving the Autobiographies a place in the prize list. *First*, It was necessary that each tale be told with a fair measure of perspicuity and intelligence; and, *Second*, breadth of representative character, fitness to afford practical suggestion and encouragement to the working-classes.

Though in revision for the press, no material alteration has been made, yet I think it proper to state that some slight additions have been given. In the first writing I felt somewhat confined. As will be seen, I had previously laboured a little in the literary vineyard, and had I mentioned any of my efforts, it would, in some cases, have been the same as giving the name, which would not have been fair to any concerned. But though I have taken a little more freedom, I know that the introduction of any new passage would not have lessened the chances of that success which crowned my attempt.

I have brought up the narrative to the present date, believing that the continuation may, in some measure, be interesting to those who feel concerned in one who has had great difficulties to contend with.

LIFE STORY.

~~~~~~

CHAPTER I.

I LEAVE the tracing of pedigrees to those who plume themselves upon the title, the rank, or the wealth of their ancestry.   With me

> " The pith o' sense, the pride o' worth,
> Are higher far than a' that."

I may remark, however, that my relations, long since dead, both on my father and mother's side, gave positive evidence of their being deeply imbued with a love of right and truth—with that genuine patriotism, that heart-felt love of country which inspires the soul of man, leads to the defence of truth, the gaining of right, and the maintaining of freedom.

I was born in Dundee, on a beautiful morning in April.   Nature seemed to rejoice with my parents, and to foster their fondest hopes.   While the homely jokes and good wishes went round the early breakfast table within the happy home, the plants were opening and the birds were singing in the green fields.   But, alas! the purest joys, like the brightest prospects, soon fade, or give way to deep sorrow and mournful wailing. Suddenly my mother felt ill.   The doctor was sent for.   She died.   I had only seen my twenty-first day when I suffered this great loss—my first misfortune—my second following hard upon the heels of the first. The wet nurse to whom I was sent was a heartless woman. To this day I suffer from the sad effects of her base treatment. Her wilful neglect and rash drugging made me a smaller and a weaker child at the end of two years than I was when my mother died. This paved the way for numerous diseases, which followed each other in rapid succession, weakening my constitution and stunting my growth.

I had but one sister, my brother, the first born, having died in childhood before I was born. My sister was about two years my senior. Having received the milk and kindness of her loving mother, and met with a better nurse than I had, she was stronger and healthier. But my condition was a source of great grief to my father. As he thought of the doings of the faithless hirelings, the idea of a second marriage entered his mind. Who could blame him? His position suggested the thought, and forced him to carry it out. This is the case with many a widower and many a widow.

Immediately after the marriage, my sister and I were taken home. From my long confinement in the cradle, the hair was worn out from the back of my head, and the skin from off my back; my very bones were wasted. But as soon as possible my position was changed from the lying to the sitting posture. Even yet I remember the size and shape of the little chair in which I sat. Just after I had seen my third birth-day, I was observed to laugh, speak, and walk, and that all in the space of a week. From this I began to grow in strength and stature till about three years after, when I had to begin to *wind*—the dreary lot of the weaver's children. I was so little, and so unfit for such sickening toil, that the feet of the *pirn-wheel* had to be cut that I might reach the spokes to drive it. There I sat, "birling" away, the wonder of many a visitor. Generally I had to drive the wheel, not of fortune, but of misery, from four in the morning till ten at night—the long day which my father had to weave hard to support his family. This gave me little refreshing sleep, less invigorating exercise, and, I may add, my food was as small in quantity and unnourishing in quality as either. No wonder though I did not become a giant in stature.

When about nine years of age, I began to feel a desire to be able to read like my father, who was one of fifteen who combined to get a copy of the *Dundee Advertiser* once a week. This was followed by the wish to be able to write, which was first created by a letter coming to us from America, where my stepmother had near relatives, all of whom loved me, and some of whom promised to send for me when I was "big"—perhaps they knew that would never be—at least I never was sent for. By what I had heard, I believed that boys in America were not wrought so hard as I was, and that they got some education, which I was not likely to get. Shortly after, I met a few scholars, who, at my request, read to me and showed me their slates and copy-books. I now urged most earnestly that I might be sent to school. At last my father consented, notwithstanding the many difficulties that stood in the way—difficulties, the strength and power of which none but the poor weaver and his suffering family can know.

Proud was I when I got my A B C card and my twopenny fee. With a heart light as the lark at rising day, I went to the school door; but imagine, if you can, my feelings as I trembled when I heard the roaring voice, the imperative command—"Hold up"—and saw the double taws make the blood spring. I had often heard of the "king of terrors," but I now thought I had seen a near relative, if not his imperial majesty. With hair standing on end I ventured in, for I was afraid to return home lest I might not get to school at all. Day after day, hatred, rage, terror, and beating were among the leading elements in this *school*. A smile from this man, *called* a teacher, would by his pupils have been regarded as one of the new wonders of the world. His theory seemed to be, what he could not cram into the head he beat into the back—a theory, I am sorry to say, yet too often put into practice by many who have higher pretensions by far than had my first teacher. He could with perfect safety have joined in the Amen to the closing part of the American Dame Teacher's speech—"It's little they gives me, and it's as little I teaches them."

Furious as this man was, and cruel as I was forced to regard him, I found he had a soft part in his heart. I became his pet; and as a token of his favour, I was asked to go for his snuff. Though he would even at times—not during school hours—doat upon me, yet I cannot say I ever loved him as a pupil ought to love a teacher. But he had a gem of a wife—a woman full of calm dignity and common sense. She interfered as frequently as possible, and often did she save the pupils from " a sarkle o' sair banes." All loved her, and nothing ever gave me more pleasure than in being able to do her the last favour she needed on earth.

After being about three months under this reign of terror, my *master* pronounced me fit for the Bible and Collection. Most gladly did I transmit the news to my father, who was under the painful necessity of taking me away from school, as there was no money to buy the books with, and as he could not want my labour longer. Though I should have been content and thankful for what I had gotten, yet I felt disappointed and grieved. Nor was my teacher ill pleased with my progress; he would frequently boast of it, giving it forth as a proof of his teaching abilities, forgetting the fact that others had been with him for as many years as I was months, and were unable to read the Primer. What aided me was my anxiety. Every second I could get from the wheel, or steal from my sleep, was intensely devoted to my book.

My father was glad to find that his effort to give a few weeks at the school was not fruitless. He felt a delight in hearing me read the little story-books which I purchased with some of the halfpennies I received from friends and others who called to see the " little winder." Though I was rather ready to take a little more than my own time in following out the magic paths of the nursery tales, my father was not now so exacting, unless he was unusually pressed. So fond did I become of the interesting stories that I acquired the habit of reading when at my meals, a habit which I have ever fostered. No miser could hunt after gold with a deeper interest than I traced the absorbing incidents in " Jack the Giant Killer," "Cock Robin," "The Babes in the Wood," and all the other popular books which I could by such means obtain. The touching tale of the hapless orphans brought tears to my eyes. Never did I love the robin-redbreast so fondly till I read how lovingly he covered the poor creatures with the forest leaves; and even yet, though I love all birds and enjoy their varied song, I confess there is a feeling towards the fairy robin which I do not experience on beholding any other of the feathered tribe.

Being favoured with a good voice, and willing to use it, I was regarded as the family reader. All the tracts, such as the *Monthly Visitor*, were reserved for Sabbath; for though the want of health and of clothes often detained my parents at home on that day, yet they respected it above all others. And let me add, this was far from being a profitless way of spending the Sabbath, of spreading the Gospel, and promoting piety. A well-intended and properly-written tract may be regarded as a messenger of mercy whithersoever it be sent, with the blessing of the Divine Master, to rouse a country to a sense of its duty, to shake the foundations of corruption, or tell the good news as proclaimed in the blessed and simple Gospel of Christ. Speaking from experience, I can say with William Howitt—" Tracts run up and down like the angels of God, blessing all, giving to all, and asking no gift in return. You can print tracts of all sizes, on all subjects, in all places, and at all hours. And they can talk to one as well as to a multitude; and to a multitude as well as to one. They require no public room to tell their story in. They can tell it in the kitchen or the shop, the parlour or the closet, in the railway carriage, or in the omnibus, or the broad highway, or in the footpath through the fields. They take no note of scoffs, or jeers, or taunts. No one can betray them into hasty or random expressions. Though they will not always answer questions, they will tell their story twice or thrice, or four times over, if you wish them. And they can be made to speak on every subject, and on every subject they may be made to speak wisely and well. They can, in short, be made vehicles of all truth; the teachers and reformers of all classes; the regenerators and benefactors of all lands."

By this means—the reading of tracts, as well as by reading the Bible—I began to think about divine things, but, of course, only as a boy would. The joy and profit which I derived from the sacred pages made me drink deeper and deeper from the blessed fountain. It was but little I could understand of the great principles of moral obligation, though simply and comprehensively laid down in the Divine Encyclopædia; yet I could, in some measure, see the soundness of its maxims, the wisdom of its precepts, and the importance of its commands. Its poetry and eloquence were to me more attractive than its philosophy and arguments; its history, its journeys, its biographies, gained from me more time and thought than its prophecies and its doctrines; yet I found in it lessons suited to my age, instruction adapted to my condition. With a hearty enthusiasm, and the tears of gratitude streaming down my pale cheeks, I would sing the sentiment in the hymn beginning—

" Holy Bible, book divine,
Precious treasure, thou art mine."

As I advanced in years, my reading began to extend. As time permitted, I had to read the newspapers aloud in my father's workshop. This became a source of income as well as information. For this new and additional employment I got a penny a-week—no small prize to a poor boy anxious to save up for some books. At this time the Reform Bill was the subject of discussion, and my father was a member of the Political Union. During that agitation there were many strong sentences made use of, calculated to arrest the attention of the inquiring young mind. These made me listen most carefully to the debates during the meal hours, and to ask many questions, such as, "What is the meaning of The Bill—the whole Bill, and nothing but the Bill?" It was then I learned my first lessons in political reform; it was then that impressions were fixed upon my mind which will never be effaced.

Young and little as I was, my seniors began to reason with me, and to impart what information they had, as if I had been an equal. So far did some of those who took an interest in me go, that they would have me walk with them in procession on the great occasion of the passing of the Reform Bill. I was sometimes led between two men, and sometimes carried upon one of their shoulders. Not being far behind the hero of the day—George Kinloch—the man whom Dundee delighted to honour—of whom that busy town will ever be proud—I saw him from my elevation, and with enthusiasm equal to any three times my age, I joined in the cry, "Kinloch for ever!" So impressed was I on that occasion, and so moved, too, when I looked upon the old man that even yet, were I an artist, I could paint his portrait.

CHAPTER II.

AN incident transpired on the occasion of this great demonstration, of which I fortunately took advantage. Mr. Smith, the manufacturer for whom my father wrought, was a true lover of civil and religious liberty; and more, he was well known as the friend of the working man. He is dead—rest to his bones and peace to his soul! None could be more anxious to honour the great event than he was. He generously treated his weavers to a dinner, in one of the public halls. I was introduced to a number of my father's fellow-workers, all of whom seemed to take a deep interest in the "little pirner," as they were pleased to call me. Their spirits being high, their hearts were generous, and each one gave me something—some a penny, some twopence, the master crowning them all by giving me half-a-crown. There was not, in my opinion, a richer man in the land than I was. Kinloch was not more elevated. This arose not so much from the mere possession of what was to me a fortune, but from the thought of what I could do with it. I had gotten a pair of trousers for the procession, and thinking I might soon obtain better clothes in which to attend church, I made a friend my banker of a sum which became the basis of what bought a suit of Sunday clothes.

Among the memorised events of my boyhood, there are none I reflect upon with more pleasure than that of getting to church. Though apparently trivial in the sight of those who walked by my side on that day, it has grown big with importance to me. The old School Wynd Church is yet a hallowed spot to me, and sacred are the hours I have spent in it. I am not sure if it was on a Fast-day or a Sabbath-day that I went first to it, but I remember the sermon was to the young, and that the subject was Christ in the Temple when he was twelve years of age. The preacher was the Rev. George Gilfillan, now one of my best and noblest friends. Through poverty, through ill report and good report, he is the same warm-hearted, sympathizing, faithful friend.

In his address, he urged his young hearers to become Sabbath scholars. I acted upon his suggestion, and regarded this as my second, if not my first step to improvement. I have every reason to thank my dear friend for his advice, the teachers for their instruction, and God for his blessing on these means. As a pupil, and as a teacher in the Sabbath-school, some of the sweetest and most pleasant associations come to my mind, giving birth to gratitude, and joy to my soul. The Sabbath-school, and my Sabbath-school teachers, will be ever dear to me. I have more than once met with one of the teachers in the first place to which I went—Mr. Robertson. I believe he is yet engaged in that holy work. A feeling of affection towards him flows from my heart when we meet. Often have I looked into the establishment of which he is one of the managers, and beheld him in silent but intense admiration. The family altar is pleasant and profitable, and may it soon be erected in every home! None who have known its benefits, and have felt its joys, will fail to keep it sacred: to see a whole family evincing an interest in their spiritual welfare, intense on their eternal salvation, is a blessed, refreshing, ennobling sight; but the Sabbath-school is needed, and especially for those who may not have the good fortune to see the family altar. The outcast or the careless may not hear the voice of Jesus, in his Word, saying, " Suffer little children to come unto me," but they may hear the invitation from the lips of the Sabbath-school teacher. I thank God I heard it.

But my getting to church, and hence to the Sabbath-school, were not the only results of the contributions from the Reformers. I had longed for a book about Wallace, and now my purse gratified my wishes. I got an old copy of " Blind Harry's " quaint rhymes. How I devoured my *new* book in old, tattered boards! My thoughts were now transferred from the hero of Dundee to the hero of Scotland. His great strength, his mighty power, his noble aim, all wrought like a charm upon my mind. Before I had gone through the book, I felt the full force of the poet's words—

" At Wallace's name, what Scottish blood
    But boils up in a spring-tide flood!"

While thus improving mentally and morally—serious impressions taking a deeper hold on my mind, the desire to be good and to do good every day increasing—I was elevated a step in the labour scale, from the wheel to the loom. My father was my apprentice-master, but, as he said, I was half-learned before I began. I was soon considered a good hand, though aided by such artificial assist-ance as clogs nailed upon the treadles to give me weight, and, by an erection below the seat-board, to give me the necessary length to reach the yarn and cloth beams.

By the time I was able to take my place with any weaver, though twice my weight, my poor father was beginning to feel the sad effects of his impaired health more severely. My first Sunday suit had vanished in tatters. This prevented me from attending church, but I stuck to my Bible and the Sabbath-school. I have gone to it in winter with bare feet and the hair sticking out of my bonnet. I often thought my poor condition made the sweet and precious words of truth which I heard sweeter and more endearing. This I have ever found to be the best source of consolation for the poor in their struggles with difficulties.

Our hard-up times were of frequent occurrence; for seldom had my father a whole week's health at once. During the best of his days, he had served his Majesty, and fought for his country as a brave British tar. Like every noble spirit, he hated tyranny in every shape, but especially that so often found on board a man-of-war. In desertion he sought relief from unprovoked and oft-repeated insult. Because of this he was denied a pension, though he of his own accord returned to the service, paid the penalty, and wrought himself up again, I believe, above the position of a common tar. At the peace he was discharged without the least acknowledgment (save a certificate of character) for the many, brave, and valuable services he had rendered to his country! Even yet I feel my blood warming when I think how he and others—those who fought our battles and won our victories—were served. It was the shameful manner in which my poor father was treated and neglected that first set my young mind against existing errors in upper quarters.

To lose his health, and bestow his energies and talents—he was a man of no ordinary abilities—in struggling to the death for his country, and yet to be steeped in misery during the remainder of his sad life was, in my opinion, very unfair, very cruel to him and his family.

So severe were our sufferings, caused by my father's ruined constitution, that I have known three weeks pass without a penny coming in, save what I wrought for. How could this keep life in a whole family? During such times of hard pressure, I have wrought twenty-four hours on end, and that on a few table-spoonfuls of pease-meal made into brose. I have heard him groaning with pain while the children were crying in vain for food. And ours was honest poverty, so far as we were concerned, but cruel poverty, so far as our country was concerned. Alas! that petty upstarts should be pampered, and that brave men should be treated as was my father. And yet some will dare ask,

"Wherefore do the poor complain?"

CHAPTER III.

PARTLY with the view of lessening the necessary domestic expenses, and partly for the benefit of health, we left the town and entered upon village life. Lochee, a place about two miles from Dundee, became our residence. But while the rent and the taxes were less, the abode was worse. It was small, low-roofed, and damp—a very grave. God help the poor! Never did the poet utter a more truthful statement when he boldly asserted that

"Man's inhumanity to man
Makes countless thousands mourn."

On every side the poor are assailed and robbed. If they are unable to pay rent for a good house, they must pay rent for a sepulchre in which to be buried alive. Our home was in the westmost but one of several apartments of an old clay building, properly called the Rotten Row, on the south side of the village.

Sickness and poverty were still our lot, but they did not extinguish my desire to learn. Amid excessive toil, I thought of " self-culture;" and I had somewhere read the couplet—

"Despair of nothing good you would attain,
Unwearied diligence your point will gain."

This induced me to hope on and work on: though often disappointed, none ever enjoyed " the pleasures of hope" better than I did.

To my great joy, in the course of time, my father recovered a little. Not now depending so much upon my labour, and knowing my desire to get on, he promised me sixpence every web I wrought, which promise he fulfilled as often as possible. This small coin emitted a beautiful ray of hope which warmed and invigorated my heart. Again the inquiry, Shall I, despite of opposing elements, taste the sweets of knowledge, and thereby become useful? suggested itself to my anxious soul; and upon this sixpence I read the words, " It is possible." From this I became more determined to grapple with every obstacle that might come in the way of attaining my object.

I felt that my pronunciation was far from being correct, and at the same time I met with an intelligent flaxdresser, who brought a second-hand copy of " Walker's Dictionary" under my notice. It was the very thing I needed, and he, being ailing and poor, was willing, and even anxious to sell it. We struck a bargain, and the dictionary became mine; it proved to be very useful.

My second book was a school Collection, every lesson in which I read most carefully, searching for the meaning and pronunciation of every word of which I felt the least uncertainty.

The third purchase was a copy-book and head-lines; and by writing a little two or three times every day I was soon able to join the letters. This enabled me to write out the meaning of the more uncommon words, which exercise I found to be most profitable, improving my spelling, and aiding me in punctuation.

Aware that a knowledge of the science of numbers was also necessary, I bought a copy of Gray's Arithmetic. I persevered for some time, but ultimately my enthusiasm began to cool down; the reason was, I had no great love for figures, nor has that little greatly increased.

But I next bought an English Grammar, and soon regained my former pitch of earnest delight. Thus I continued, reading in the night time, often when others were asleep; writing in the meal-hours, while others were gossiping or romping; and learning arithmetical tables and rules of grammar when weaving, the books being fastened on the lay or breast-beam. When there was no extra pressure I was as regular as the clock, from six A.M. till ten P.M. During these hours I went over no little work for my strength; and, as a rule, I imposed upon myself a certain portion of work every hour, and when that was finished before the hour was done, I would rest and read till the time expired. I devoted these snatches to reading speeches and lectures of the great agitators of the day—a species of reading in which I took great delight, and from which I derived much profit.

Encouraged by my comparative success, and urged by the hope of greater achievements, I now sought the aid of a living voice to tell me if my advances were genuine. Mr. Auchterlonie was the teacher to whom I applied: he had a good heart, and his abilities were of no ordinary nature: he felt a delight in his pupils, and was delighted to see them getting on. It was fortunate that I met with such a feeling man and willing teacher.

For a time I attended his evening class; he was proud of my progress; but again I felt a check in the renewed illness of my father. Poor man, he suffered long and sorely. Shortly after he got better, an addition was made to the family. Well do I remember the morning on which the young visitor came. Though my parents may be well classed among the sober, yet they so far acted in accordance with the absurd drinking customs of society as to have the dram in the house at births as well as deaths. I was sent to the publican's with the bottle—an errand I did not much like; for though there was not then a Band of Hope, I was beginning to believe in the doctrine of taste and handle not the unclean thing. As is generally the case with the poor who have but one apartment, on such occasions the family are roused up early in the morning, and sent anywhere to be out of the way. I was wearied, ill-clad, cold, and hungry; and the spirit-dealer had over-slept, so that I had to stand long at his door before he came, while the sleet lashed upon my bare feet and half-uncovered head. When I came home, the nurse—who was a giant in stature, and in heart, I thought, like a stone—drove me forth with a basin of cold brose in hand for my break-fast. A sham prudence gave a pretext for this harsh treatment; but I could not but think that if my mother had been alive no iron-hearted wretch would have been allowed to send me off so cold, so hungry, and so heart-broken. Of course, I could not eat, though like to faint. I was about half-way in my teens, and gene-rally regarded as manly—"though little"—yet I wept like a child, and sought a quiet nook wherein to pour out my grief. I took to rhyming, and the first four verses of the following "wail" was the result. I felt relief after this expression of my sorrow. It pleased my boyish fancy, and I thought and wished I was destined to become a poet. After this, when I thought myself ill-used, I took to writing verse, in which I found no small solace. This piece being my first at-tempt, and it having been frequently honourably mentioned, I give it here:—

MY MAMMY'S AWA'.

Cauld, cauld is the day, the frost nips my wee face;
I'm heartless and sad, how waefu' my case !
On my bare wee leggies the bitin' winds blaw—
Oh ! hoo is a' this ? My Mammy's awa' !

Baith laddies an' lassies are happy an' gay,
They rin to the schule and then to their play;
But I maun rin errants 'mang frost, sleet, an' snaw—
Oh ! hoo is a' this ? My Mammy's awa' !

They a' get braw claes an' their head fu' o' lear,
To mak' them a' great, if God should them spare,
But nae schulin' for me, nae learnin' ava—
Oh! hoo is a' this? My Mammy's awa'!

But I'll always push on to get lear like the lave,
I'll ever be active, determined, an' brave;
Tho' hard be my fate, it safter may blaw—
For God will prove kind, tho' Mammy's awa'!

For yet she looks doon frae the far land o' bliss,
Aye langin' to gi'e me a mother's fond kiss,
An' watching my footstaps to husit or ha',
So I'll aye be happy, tho' Mammy's awa'!

Oh, yes! her loved spirit tho' wafted on high,
Will follow me aye till I mount to the sky;
Oh! gin I were there, I wid fear nane ava,
For God will be there, an' Mammy an' a'!

When my father became better to do, he generously and thoughtfully proposed that I should pay only for my bed and board, and have what I made besides to enable me to make more progress in my aspirations. This offer was accepted with thanks, and my exertions, means, and knowledge increased. I thought I was now in a fair way to reach the summit of my ambition—the pulpit. I wrought hard almost night and day, in order to save as much as would pay a month's board in advance, that I might get to the day-school. This I accomplished, to my great joy. Mr. Auchterlonie had left the place, but it was now well supplied by Mr. Doctor, a man equally able, ready, and anxious to help those who wished to advance. He was well-versed in various branches of learning, and had a ready aptitude in teaching what he knew. He soon became much interested in me, and did his best to help me on. To the branches in which I had already made some progress, I added the study of geography, grammar, &c.; but this working and learning was far beyond my strength. Nature seized me as a lawless offender, and stopped my imprudent career for a time. The dangerous illness (inflammation) had often laid me low before, but the attack was never so severe. My unexpected recovery gave rise to the idea in my mind that I had been preserved for some particular purpose—at least to be useful; and hence, as soon as I was able, I began to think, and work, and learn, as before.

But I could not be idle during my convalescence. I read three works which were kindly lent to me by friends who were anxious to feed my inquiring mind. The books were of great service to me; they not only engendered new ideas, but they gave animation to feelings which from time to time had been planted in my mind from what I had previously read, seen, or heard. The "Scottish Worthies" was the first I read; and the many manly and heroic deeds therein so graphically narrated will never be erased from my mind. The strong hearts, the noble aims, the indomitable resolution, the almost frantic enthusiasm of these heroes, stamped an impression upon my heart that will remain long in my memory: their glorious deeds won my admiration, and their intense sufferings awakened my sympathy. Often did I pause and tremble when reading these stirring records of the hot and savage times. What a glorious idea, thought I to myself, to see the rich and poor, the learned and unlettered, asserting the right to think for themselves, rising in fearless honesty against oppression, and bravely vindicating, to the death, the liberty of the human conscience!—to see them manfully paying the stern penalty of their burning love towards eternal truth!—to see them

"Still pressing onward, red-wat shod,"

to victory or death, and at last dying in hope, in faith, and in the sweet peace of believing!

The beautiful and majestic story of the "Pilgrim's Progress" was of another stamp, but no less interesting. Tell a boy in his teens that that work is a fiction, and he will not readily believe you. It becomes doubly interesting after one has earnestly commenced his homeward journey to the better land. The great novel is a great fact —a splendid conception, well wrought up by the noble pilgrim himself—a book alike for old and young, and for all conditions and positions in life.

And as for Burns, the Bard, how I read, and laughed, and wept! I felt proud when I thought he was a Scotsman; and I earnestly wished that I might be able to evince even a tenth-part of his vast, rich, glowing, and overflowing genius. There was such a charm about what he said that I was almost falling in love with *all* he said, even with his errors. There was also something in my circumstances at the time that made me more ready to swallow his bitter things. Happily, I had experienced the religious feelings so eloquently, graphically, and so touchingly expressed in his "Cottar's Saturday Night;" and I had seen a specimen of, and had suffered from, the hypocrisy which withered under his cutting satire. I admired, nay almost worshipped the poet, but wept for the man.

CHAPTER IV.

AFTER I was again able to work, my first great effort was to clear off debts contracted during my illness. This was not an easy task; but it had to be done. The doctors were the most easily paid. The strange and serious nature of my past distress made it the subject of talk in the village. Dr. Wood—a good man and a skilful physician—was called in. For long the disease baffled his efforts. Dr. Henry—a clever but unfortunate man, since drowned—heard of the case, and kindly offered his services by way of visiting, consulting, and advising with Dr. Wood so many times a day. Both were equally generous towards me. Dr. Henry would not take anything for all he did; neither would Dr. Wood, he only taking ten shillings for all the medicine he had given during the time!

But this was not the only proof of his thoughtful kindness. He also manifested a desire to forward me in my studies, lending me his medical and chemical books, and giving me instruction in these valuable sciences. I became his pupil, and was often with him. But he died, and many, as well as I, lamented his sudden departure. I am happy to say his first lessons were not lost; they led me to wish for more, and I believe induced me long after to pay more attention to medicine and its influence on disease.

Shortly after I was again able to stand upright and attend my classes as before, labour generally, and the weaving particularly, came to a fearful discount. Most of the work entrusted to the vil·

lage agents was withdrawn, and wages were soon
reduced to the point of starvation.

In the midst of this want and misery, the country was agitated from one end to the other; and
worse still, the Corn-law Repealers and the
Chartists—forgetting the very instructive application of Æsop's fable of the lion and the four
bulls—were foolishly contending with each other,
while the common foe was fiendishly laughing
at their insane folly. The stratagems of the
enemies of right and truth are various, and often
subtle; but that of fomenting jealousies, to create
hatred and aversion among the sufferers, is generally resorted to. It too frequently causes separation and contentions; and never was this base
device more successful than at the time to which
I refer.

In common with many more, I was convinced
that something should be done to check the starvation which was sending thousands to premature
graves. I also believed in the propriety of re-
pealing the Corn Laws, thinking that such might
give a temporary relief to a hungry nation; but
I was also convinced there was a deeper wrong
than a dear loaf and the want of work, and many
since, though then opposed to that opinion, have
borne testimony to its truthfulness. That docu-
ment known as "the People's Charter" gained
my approval, and I joined the National Chartist
Association. This brought me into contact with,
and in some cases pitted me against, the Corn-
law Repealers, some of whom had the power, and
not a few the will, to deprive me of the ordinary
chances of labour. I shall only mention one
example: There were only three or four manu-
facturers in the village. One of them was fortu-

nate enough to get an order for some work I had wrought for him before, and he told the foreman to give me a web. How glad I was even of the promise! With the rest I waited my turn, calling every day; and how the foreman did his best to tease me! He not only kept me coming and going, for his own gratification, till every web was given out; but he then, with a cowardly sneer, told me to go and live on the "charter." By his kind, this was thought "wut;" by right-thinking people it would have been regarded as punishable cruelty. I need not trace the sad effects of this disappointment in the family; but when I looked into my father's face, and upon the hungry family around me, I could have sought vengeance, had I acted according to my first thoughts. But the time-serving fellow not being within my reach, and not being in posses-sion of the necessary physical strength to chastise him, I only asked, in bitterness,

> "Why has man the will and power
> To make his fellow mourn?"

Such attempts to lead me to change my opinions, or rather to screw me out of existence, made me the more given to opposition when opportunity afforded. I was elected Secretary to the Lochee Branch of the National Chartist Association. I also ventured, young as I was, to move or second resolutions at public meetings held in the village. I have not forgotten the agitated state of my mind during the delivery of my maiden speech. I could not see my audience. Of course there was plenty of cheering from the Chartists, and hooting and yelling from the

Repealers, and I got to the end amid applause. But I soon became firm enough to meet an antagonist any night, and I did enjoy the fun. Really, if hunger had kept away, the excitement was so great that one would not have wearied during the dull times.

There was many a laughable scene in the Weaver's Hall. Once the Chartists were to be convinced, by the chief of the village, of their folly in asking a vote for every man, because he was a man, in the true sense of the word—the head and front of my offence. The hall was crowded; and such a hubbub! The orator began thus :—"Gentlemen, I have an important task to perform. I have not had time to *study a speech*, but I would say all should become Repealers just now." A voice—"So we are." "Why are you Chartists, then?" A voice—"Because we want the right of voting." "Do you not want a repeal of the Corn Laws?" A voice—"Yes, and the power to sweep off every other bad law, and place good ones in their stead." "Then, we are one." "Would you give a moral and sensible man, if full age, a vote?" "If he paid a ten pound rent." Here followed shouts of derisive laughter from the great mass, and hear, hear, from a few of the ten pounders.

Supposing the *gentleman* to have finished his speech, I went to the platform, and was about to offer a few remarks, when he protested, saying he had not yet begun! I gave way, and he stood conceiving, but brought forth nothing. Finding his memory and nerves rather weak, he looked behind him for his hat, in which he expected to find the MS. of the unprepared speech, but, lo! no speech was there, and he, poor fellow, had to sit down, amid long and continued laughter. I followed, and pitched into him. His weakness gave me strength and courage.

I next became a correspondent for the village to a newspaper established in Dundee, for the advocacy of the principles which I professed. Between this, the secretaryship, the preparing of speeches, and being a member of the Dundee Democratic Council, I had plenty to do, but nothing for it. Even when I had work I kept a sharp eye after every movement in the village, and reported accordingly. What has that little devil in the paper this week? was among the first questions put by those who feared me, when the newspaper appeared in Lochee. Having become quite fearless, I lashed what I conceived to be the wrong, and upheld what I regarded as right.

Hunger and misery came to the unbearable point. Dundee was in commotion, and Lochee was nearly as bad. A public meeting was held on the Magdalen Green. It is said that nearly ten thousand were present. The question was, What were the unemployed to do for themselves and their families? Various were the opinions expressed by the leaders. A demonstration was at last agreed to, and, on the Monday following, acted upon. My father wisely prevented me from being at this meeting; but though a strict watch was kept after me, I managed to escape and join the hungry mob at the Fair Muir, on their way to Forfar.

On Monday night we encamped about mid-way between Dundee and Forfar. On arriving at the outskirts of the County Town, we were met by an array of constables, baton in hand. After a few explanations, the black wall of opposition was split in two, and through we marched in triumph!

When we arrived at the place appointed, crowds gathered about us. Some one mentioned my name: it is a rare one, but being long well known in Forfar—my father and grandfather's natal spot—it attracted the attention of some around me. A number of questions were put to me; I became a favourite, and was taken to a first-rate homely tea breakfast, which was thankfully received.

But I was not the only one to whom the Forfarians, especially the women, were kind. It was a treat to behold the latter, as well as to enjoy their kindness in time of need. Though it was early in the morning, they were as neat and clean as if they had been preparing for strangers, or going to meet their sweethearts. They wore heavy, but neat shoes, stout wincey petticoats, and buff shortgowns, the sleeves of which were so nicely turned up, that the plump, well-formed arm was seen to advantage. In form they were sturdy, yet handsome, and a beautiful fresh and rosy face shone out from a pure white cap with double border. They were very attractive, and would have made a delicious photographic group, until some of them opened their mouths to speak. It was not their teeth that were wrong; no, as a general rule, they were white and well-set; it was the tongue that was faulty. There were some exceptions, but one was led to think that Forfar kept a swearing master. I was sorry to be forced to this conclusion, and even yet I would hope the roughness of expression was only the result of a bad example, and bad habits, not of bad hearts. Every one evinced good and tender hearts; each did her best for the rebel race.

The magistrates vied with the ladies in acts of kindness towards us. They that morning improved the maxim, "Better flatter fools than fight with them." Instead of *flattering* they *fed* us with beer and baps. This had the desired effect. What the poor creatures wanted was work and food. At ten o'clock a large meeting was held, but the speeches were less exciting than those delivered in the fields under the midnight canopy. Fear had evidently taken hold of the leaders—the blind leaders of the blind—and their followers were also beginning to see their error. All thought of returning home, *if they could get.* It was reported, and with truth, that policemen and constables were stationed at every avenue to Dundee, for the purpose of apprehending the "rebels" [?] as they approached. Conscious that I had neither intended nor done ill—and I believe most of the others were in the same position—I took courage, and boldly passed the sentries. Dundee was in a state of great excitement. Some of the policemen seemed anxious for a disturbance. Nothing but the good sense of the people saved the town from a fearful riot.

When I arrived in Lochee, I found my enemies doing what they could to get me imprisoned, by telling lies, and some of them offering to swear to their false statements. My relatives being alarmed, and believing I could not, at that time, get work, though there had been plenty, I left the village in search of employment, and until the ire of my cowardly foes should be cooled down.

CHAPTER V.

WHEN I became the poor wanderer from place to place, a shirt and a few books were my only moveables, all of which had soon to be sold to supply my wants. Before I got regular employment, I endured much. Under the dark clouds of despair, and suffering very keenly from the sickening pangs of hunger, often did I resolve to end my days, by taking away the few sparks of life that remained; but an unknown voice called out, "Hold! trust a little longer; lean on the anchor of hope." I do not know how I lived, nor what I existed upon. I shall only mention one case of many.

When leaving Montrose for Brechin, I possessed only one penny. An hour before I left, I felt very hungry, and bought gingerbread. The half of it was all I could take, and I kept the other for a future repast; but I was not far on the way when I met a beggar and some children, all of whom seemed to be more in want of a piece than I was. They got my poor store, and on I travelled, till the dark mantle of night enveloped me. How dreary the road was! and I was as "dowie an' wae." Again I felt the pangs of hunger—pangs, the pains and keenness of which can only be known to those who have felt them. I sank down by the wayside. My spirit and heart failed with my body. While in this almost insensible state, "nature's soft nurse" (dear creature!) came up, threw her gentle arms around me, and carried me to the land of dreams. There I remained for a short time, after which I found myself again resting upon the hard, be-dewed roadside. I felt bewildered, and did not know what direction to take; but a man came up, bound for Brechin. I spoke to him. He slackened his pace, and we went on together, arriving early in the morning.

I found the man to whom I had a note of introduction, but he, too, had been long idle from want of work. He did not mention breakfast to me, but I suppose the poor man had nothing to spare. He gave me the name of a friend in Luthermuir, a village seven miles east of Brechin, and nine north of Montrose. By this time my limbs could scarcely support me, but I travelled on as well as I could. By the time I arrived, I had been thirty-two hours without food, save the mouthful of gingerbread.

Here, too, I found the person upon whom I called nearly as poor as myself, only he and his family were at home. They did their best for me, and more than they were well able. They had the heart, and that helped them to find the way. What would the poor do were it not for the poor? I asked myself as this kind man and his family received me in the spirit of a Christian. The very sight of food was too much for my weak state. A severe and almost deadly sickness deprived me of the power of seeing and hearing for a time. Those around me thought grim death was fast approaching. As soon as I was able, in answer to various questions, I openly told the state I was in, and gave some slight idea of what I had endured. It is said the real Scotsman would always be independent, if possible; he would almost sooner starve than beg—ever suffer-ing greatly before he confesses his poverty, however honest. I confess I was touched with this spirit. I would have had many a meal I wanted had I told how matters stood. On this occasion I tried to strike the medium, and reveal a part of my sufferings.

By the generous kindness of my new friends, I began in a day or two to recover somewhat from the direful effects of fatigue and hunger. For three weeks before I arrived there was not a web in Luthermuir. A large number were in a state of starvation; but they were in high hopes that night, and they were not disappointed. The carts came from Montrose, and brought a web for all who sought it, and one to spare for " the poor stranger," as they called me. The people said I had brought God's blessing with me.

The fabrics there were very fine, and of dazzling whiteness. When I received my web and weft I did not know how to act, the kind was so different from what I had been accustomed to weave; but as soon as my new shop-mates observed that I was so far behind, they, without waiting to be asked, rendered every necessary assistance. The kind creatures, both men and women, aided me from the best of motives—simply because I was needing their help. I got on well, and was soon able to do as much, and make as good work as any. At the end of the first month I got some clothing; at the end of the second I was able to send something home to help my father; and at the end of the third I returned home, healthy and well clad.

When leaving, a large number of my friends escorted me a mile or two on my way. My heart was filled with emotion, and the tears of gratitude ran down my cheeks. I shall ever remember with pleasure the kindness I received at the hands of my warm-hearted friends in Luthermuir.

As soon as I arrived in Lochee my old acquaintances came round about me, to bid me welcome; but my old foes felt as if they wished I had rather not come; they were actually afraid of me, yet I am sure I never injured one of them by word or deed; I simply defended what I conceived to be truthful and proper in the cause I had earnestly espoused. Those who know anything of the state of the country at that time will not be astonished that a youth—poverty stricken, yet full of hope—persecuted, yet enthusiastic, as I was—should have taken an active part in any movement promising liberty and better times. And yet there are some narrow enough in mind to deny me my ordinary and admitted chances of success, because of my juvenile honesty of purpose and hearty earnestness!

As soon as possible, I bought more books, and retraced my studies with care. But some time after this a change came over my mind, not for the better, and which cost me many an anxious hour. From the time I went to the Sabbath-school till the time I became a poor wanderer, I had wished and hoped to become a preacher of the gospel. I had longed for the learning necessary; not that I ever believed in the virtue of serving so many years as an apprentice to the great and good work. I wished to get to the Colleges and Halls for the sake of what knowledge could be had there, and for the sake of the training and its benefit. But circumstances had almost crushed that hope, and poverty had prevented me from getting to the church, to the Sabbath-school, or to the minister's (Rev. D. Marshall) class for a long period. From the time I left home, till some time after my return, I had not seen a minister, a missionary, nor an elder who spoke to me on divine matters. Nor was I alone in this respect. Much has been said, and much has been done on foreign stations by zealous missionaries, and it is most gratifying to know that God is blessing their labours; but, oh! there was, and is, a sad need for such efforts at home. I admit good is being done, but I hold much more should be done in that direction. Looked upon as an outcast, treated by the professedly religious as if I had no soul to be saved, I became doubtful as to whether or not there was what some called Christianity; and at this time I was induced to become a member of a debating society, a few members of which were called believers, but the majority were professed infidels; indeed, the words " We atheists" were frequently uttered in a tone of haughty pride. Though many of them were clever, and some gave proofs of talent, yet I could not help thinking at times that the Scottish adjective " wee" might have suited better than the personal pronoun "we." They were very anxious to get me advanced (?) to their standard, and for that purpose lent me many of their books, some of which possessed an intellectual grandeur which I could not but admire, and their profuse glitter had an influence on my mind. As most young people foolishly do, I had begun to look at Christianity through its professors, and these books made the mote and beam. Viewing Christianity through such a bad medium, I unjustly concluded that it had no divine foundation, because, as I then thought, it was without any good influence; and I was judging from what I had seen and experienced, as well as from what I read and heard. There were noble exceptions; but the most I had as yet met with who professed to be religious, I had known to be anything but loving and lovable —anything but honest and charitable—anything but what they tried to make men believe they were; they were kirk folks on Sabbath, and unjust folks throughout the week—God's children, by pretension, for fifty-two days a year, and the devil's, by practice, for the remaining three hundred and thirteen. All this, and the fact of the great national suffering existing, and which I regarded as the result of political and social wrong, in a Christian country, confirmed my rather hastily drawn conclusion.

Though I still continued, in the midst of conflicting notions and discussions on such topics as " The existence of a God," and " The authenticity of the Bible," to entertain the noblest ideas regarding the being and character of God, yet I was very unhappy while in this doubting and fault-finding state of mind. I passed many an anxious and sleepless night. I felt as if I could have given the world, had it been mine, if that would have made me the devout youth, earnest in matters of religion, that I once was. Whatever blame might have been laid to my account, I know this, and God knows it too, that the conduct of hypocrites, and the want of Sabbath clothes, brought round this state of mind, which, but for the providence of God, might have made me miserable here and hereafter; and even yet, while I have to thank God I have no longer any doubts as to the divine origin and real power of the principles of that Christianity given out by Christ and his apostles, I have reason to fear that the greatest and worst enemies with which love, truth, and right have to contend, are the deceitful and base who, under false colours, have gotten within the Church; I fear, I say, many who profess to acknowledge the Most High—to believe and obey His Word—are the greatest foes to the glory of God, and hence to the happiness of man.

In going through this dangerous ordeal I lost something and I gained something; I lost, and never have I entirely regained, that child-like devotion which I had so long and so happily enjoyed. I bless God I escaped as I did; and I thank him, too, that what I before believed simply because my parents or my Sabbath-school teachers said it, I again believed because I had, as well as I could, examined for myself. And now the folly and errors and evil consequences of infidelity were to me more apparent than ever; and hence the desire to proclaim the good news of salvation to man took a stronger hold of my mind, and has never left it since.

During this mental conflict I did not forget my studies. I had advanced so far that the teacher would entrust me with the charge of his evening classes; and I experienced an agreeable feeling when he would send his pupils to me for help, saying, I could aid them as well as he could. This gained for me the title of " The Helper," and the advancement increased my hopes of becoming a teacher. With this view I took private lessons from celebrated teachers, among whom was Mr. (now Rev.) George Hunter. He had known something of the " pursuit of knowledge under difficulties," and his " fellow-feeling " made him " wondrous kind." He introduced me to the

Literary Institute, of which he was a member, and which I joined about two years after.

After keeping an evening class for some time, another attack of inflammation laid me up. The doctor scolded, blaming my weaving during the day, teaching in the evening, and studying in the night, as the cause of my distress; but my pupils paid up their fees, and I got to the country as soon as I could walk. When I came home I was more cheerful than ever. I was enabled to continue my preparations for becoming a public instructor, by being employed in several families as a private teacher.

CHAPTER VI.

ON 25th November, 1844, I opened a school at Smithfield, a small plot of houses at the top of Hilltown, Dundee. I did not begin "under distinguished patronage," neither did I make any great pretension. The small bill announcing my opening, simply held out that I was to teach reading, writing, and arithmetic. Latin and mathematics were not mentioned, because they were not needed, and because I knew but little of either—at least, I could not profess to teach them. I have ever detested quackery, and of all kinds palmed on the public, there is none more contemptible than that which too often springs from the vanity of young men becoming teachers. With few exceptions they try to make the credulous believe they possess great learning.

whereas, in not a few cases, they should attend
to the advice,

> "Let all the foreign tongues alone,
> Till you can read and spell your own."

I began with ten pupils, at the fee of twopence
each per week. But the smallness of income was
not my only difficulty. The other teachers endeavoured to throw contempt upon my humble
seminary, by calling it " The Laddie's School."
This was puerile, certainly, and my age, stature, and dress gave a kind of pretext for their
small spite; but the result proved that positive good may come from apparent evil. The
ridicule thrown upon my efforts wrought for
the benefit of my pupils, as well as myself.
When any urchin became a habit-and-repute
truant, he, as a punishment, was sent to "The
Laddie's School." The foolish boys and thought-
less girls tried my temper, but they also made
me begin the study of the means of imparting
instruction to them, and of gaining their affections. To my joy, and the advantage of my
charge, I succeeded beyond expectation. But
scarcely had I, in some measure, overcome the
opposition of my fellow-teachers, when a minister
came to their rescue, and brought all his influence to bear against me. Some of the parents,
who reasoned that if I conquered and improved
the truants, I would also benefit the well-to-do,
belonged to his church; and he could not bear
the idea of any pupils going past the school in
connection with his church. Some yielded to
his injunctions, but the most afterwards confessed,
when bringing their children back to me, that
they had taken a wrong step. The minister still
lives, but is not now in that district.

During the first three months of my teaching, I had not five shillings a-week for my labour. I was in want of three things—food, clothes, and books, and to get these tested my wits. I arranged with my father, who by this time had left Lochee, to pay a portion of his rent for my bed, and to board myself. This I did to have an opportunity of weaving late at night and early in the morning, without any one knowing of it save the family; for, strange to say, had the public known I was put to such shifts, I might have closed my school-door. I had soon to give up this weaving by stealth. I had but one suit, and, all I could brush, there was no possibility of getting rid of the weaver's livery when going to school. The truth is, I was little the better of my effort; for by the time the web was wrought, the money was needed for the house, and my share was small.

This effort having failed, another had to be made. If possible a more rigid economy had to be exercised. If the mind was to be fed, or the back clothed, it must be done at the expense of the stomach. I now resolved to make my meals in the school-room. A small kettle, a jug, and a spoon served my purpose. I entered the school-room early in the morning, studied till nine, supped my pease-brose, took a smell of the fresh air, and after a race or a game with my pupils, entered at ten on the labours of the day. Between one and two o'clock, I kept a class for grown-up females. At five I took some coffee and a biscuit; then read till seven, when I went to get some private lessons; returning at nine, took a little brose, studied till eleven, and went to bed.

The only variation from this course was when

my enthusiasm made me forget myself and remain longer at night than my set time; and one Sabbath, when I went twice or thrice to church, and studied religious subjects—collecting Bible facts, &c., for my pupils. From the first, I considered it my duty to teach Christian precepts, and not sectarian doctrines, as well as general knowledge. I never could see the propriety, nor even the possibility, of separating the sacred from the secular branches of a common school education. Moral training is as necessary as intellectual facts; and hence our teachers should not only be intelligent men and women, but enlightened Christians. It may be held that this rule cannot be applied to seminaries where only one or two branches, such as mathematics, are taught; but I contend at present for its full and free application in public schools for the masses.

At the end of my first session, I was in possession of some educational works, and about forty shillings. I had longed to visit Edinburgh, and I now resolved to see "The City of Palaces." I enjoyed the beautiful and striking sight which the magnificence of the Scottish capital presents to the inquiring stranger. The lion-like Arthur's Seat, and the time-defying Salisbury Crags struck me with amazement; but I lingered longest on the Calton Hill, the monuments upon which made me think of the moral and intellectual greatness and usefulness of the mighty dead. Among the conspicuous erections which dot this hill is a group of twelve gigantic pillars, called the *National Monument*. Some regret that the want of funds prevented the finishing of this building; but whatever may be said of the want of public spirit, I am convinced the erection, as it is, answers the original purpose better than if it had been completed. Many a gigantic scheme has been planned, yet, whoever saw the project completely gained by war? But, as if to relieve the sad reflections, produced by beholding this "stuck" monument to the warriors, within the area of where the edifice was intended to be, is Forrest's Statuary, a self-erected monument to the genius, skill, and perseverance of a great artist. It was to me an attractive exhibition, one which I have again and again seen, always with increased delight.

After visiting the various institutions and interesting places, I left for home, to teach and be taught as before. I had a fair opening, and, to the day, I added an evening class. To my joy and profit I had become more popular during my month's vacation. The teacher to whom I went for private lessons had other teachers as his pupils. This was the first means of introducing me to the cloth. Some began to visit me on the Saturdays "to see what was in me," as they phrased it; and others, with the noble motive of giving me the right hand of fellowship, and wishing me God-speed. Among the latter, I would, in gratitude, mention names—the old and able teacher, Mr. Macintosh, author of several worthy productions—Mr. Hamilton, the successful teacher at Meadowside—and Mr. Campbell, teacher of English, &c., in the public seminaries, and author of several useful school and other books. I was much indebted to the advice and encouragement handsomely and generously given by these men, at a time when it was much needed.

To my surprise and delight, I was asked to allow myself to be proposed as a member of the Forfar, Perth, and Fifeshire Teachers' Association. Though I felt honoured by this mark of respect, I saw my inferiority the more by coming often in contact with the learned and polite. Their conversation was interesting as well as instructive; and though I preferred to be a "hearer" rather than a "doer," yet every time I left the meetings I entered on the work of self-improvement with renewed energy. At first I felt rather uneasy, never having been in polite circles before; but the greatest difficulty I experienced in this way was on the occasion of the Society's Annual Dinner in the Royal Hotel. The greater body of the teachers from the three counties, the Provost, the Bailies, George Duncan, M.P., and other influential gentlemen, were present; and I was timid enough; but I remembered the moral of the lesson called " The Bashful Man's Account of Himself," and fortunately I was placed next to Mr. Duncan, who was of great service to me.

About this time I formed the acquaintanceship of some young men of a literary turn of mind, and became a member of their Society, then known, I think, as " The Literary Emporium." I had read little save books on the art of teaching, and others which had a tendency to advance me in my profession. Seeing my deficiency, I bore a low sail for a time, but ultimately took a share in the debates, and even read an essay now and then. There was little mercy shown in criticising my first attempt; but I felt the better of a little sharpening up, and spent many a pleasant and profitable evening amid our battles.

Among the few with whom I thus associated was James Scrymgeour—clever, strange, fast, and, no doubt, well-intended—hearty in his love and fiery in his hatred. We fought often, especially after I began to assert my equality with him as a member of the Society. Often did he say, in a joke, of course, "It is my work to level hillocks;" but with all our shortcomings and bickerings there was something akin in us which kept us united, if not in love, at least in friendship. I love him to this day; and never shall I forget the mutual pleasure we have had at tea, in rambles, and in "The Halls of Lamb."

Next in the succession of events was an unexpected examination of my school. How this came about, I know not, but the public were pleased to find the result to be for my good. One Saturday evening an elder called and asked me if I would permit a deputation from the Dundee Presbytery of the Church of Scotland to examine my school. In a moment I consented. He told me they were coming on the Monday following, at eleven o'clock. This was rather unusual, and the parents felt it, because of the want of longer notice, to get their children dressed. The Rev. Mr. Logan, who took the lead, cleared me of any blame, and told the parents who came that the Presbytery wished to see the school in its real everyday working order. This was backed up by the Rev. Mr. (now Principal) Tulloch, and others. The examination went on for three hours. At the close, I was gratified to hear the hearty expressions of approbation from every minister present. They were pleased to say that my system of instruction was not only new, but an improvement upon the old.

Chapter VII.

From this, my school began to fill. In the district, one teacher after another gave way, until I became "the mester." The last one, before he left, was reduced to seven pupils, with whom he called one Monday, and said to me, "Now, sir, since you have taken the rest, you are welcome to these." I thanked the gentleman, and took in the seven, who received a hearty welcome from my pupils.

The decks being cleared, and I being now somewhat successfully and favourably introduced into public life, I received invitations from parents and others. I uniformly declined, but devoted an hour each evening to regular visitation of *all* the parents and guardians of my scholars. I saved them the unnecessary trouble of "preparing for the teacher," and I saw things as they were, by not saying upon whom nor when I was to call. This is a plan I would humbly recommend to every teacher of a Public School. The more he knows of the condition and habits of parents and children, the better for all concerned. None knows the good that is likely to rise out of a friendly visit, even to oneself. I shall here mention three incidents in point which had their origin in my visitations to the parents of my pupils.

Though one may try, as I always did, to show no respect of persons, either to pupils or their parents, yet there are always a few to whom you can speak with more freedom, and who show a greater interest in you than others. In more cases than one, I experienced this. There was a clean, thrifty, and sensible mother, who was blessed with a sober and steady husband. She had a young and numerous family. It was not easy for them to get ends to meet. But they made that out and paid the teacher too. I was a favourite of hers, and she took a deep interest in me. On one of my visitings, she spoke to me about her minister in such a friendly way that I was induced to go and hear him—the Rev. (now Dr.) James R. M'Gavin. I liked him. There was something so pleasing about his manner, so attractive in his delivery, so musical in his voice, so choice in his words, and so instructive in his matter, that I attended on his ministry and became a member of his Church; and continued so, with pleasure and profit, till I had to leave for a country school for the sake of regaining health. He proved to be a good friend to me.

The other incident was also important to me. A sweet girl, named Aggie, was among my first pupils. Her father was not of the ordinary stamp of minds. He had read a good deal, and had elevated ideas of teaching, at least so far as intellectual facts, and the mode of teaching them, were concerned. He had often expressed a wish to meet me, and I was anxious to have a conversation with him. On the afternoon I called, a female relative from Edinburgh was there on a visit. Aggie called her "Aunty Maggie." The visitor took very little part in the conversation, but she watched, with quiet delight, the movements of her dear bewitching, and constantly chatting, niece; now clinging to me, and then looking into my face, as only an endearing and affectionate girl could do—her little sister trying to follow her example. "Aunty Maggie," said I to myself, "there is something truly charming in the name." So much so that I could not help taking a sly peep into her lovely face. A soft ray from her beaming eyes touched my heart, kindled that spark in my soul called love—a spark which can only go out with the lamp of life. She was Aggie's favourite aunt, and she is now the dear wife of my bosom. I bless the day I first saw her; and to this day, Aggie—she who led me that night to the house—has a hold of my affections only second to my own dear, beautiful children.

The third incident to which I refer is not without its value, not only to me, but, I hope, to others. I visited the parents of five children, two of whom were at my school. The mother was at home, and after talking with her for some time on general matters, and the children and their schooling in particular, she gave a look in which there was a meaning, to the eldest girl, who immediately went to the "press," took something from it, and went out. In a short time she came back, replaced the something where she took it from, and began to prattle away as if she had done nothing. I saw this as if I saw it not; but when I made signs of leaving, the mother said, "na, na, mester, ye maun taste wi's afore ye leave," and taking the bottle from the press, offered me a glass of whisky. The woman had an honest face, and, no doubt, a kind heart. Her children, too, were promising, but one was without stockings. "Might not that sixpence, just spent for whisky to treat me, have helped to buy a pair for the girl?" asked I at myself. I knew the woman was taking the usual mode of showing her respect towards me, and, in my heart, I thanked her; but she did not know at what sacrifice the proof of her kindly disposition was manifested. " These drinking habits," thought I, "rob the children, and teach them bad lessons." I did taste the spirits, but gave the youngest child sixpence, and resolved from that moment *never to give nor take intoxicating drinks as a token of friendship or hospitality*. I have kept my resolution, and I pray God I may ever act upon it, both for my own and for others' sake. This was my first lesson in abstinence from strong drink.

At this time I had never read a book nor a pamphlet on the Temperance question, nor did I join the society for two or three years afterwards. But I have since carefully studied the nature and tendency of intoxicating drinks, the danger and injury of our drinking habits, and the more I examine and reflect, the more clearly I see the necessity of abstinence; and I rejoice the more that I resolved so early to abstain, not that I undervalue alcohol when in its proper place. Its power as a medicine is great, and, if skilfully managed, often beneficial. Like every other poison, it is dangerous, and often deadly, when out of its place. Dr. Gregory told the truth when he said—" I never got a patient by water drinking, but thousands by strong liquors." This goes far to prove two important points:—1. That perfect health is compatible with total abstinence; 2. That alcoholic liquors induce disease, and thereby human misery, and premature death. But though this is an indisputable fact, I will not at present attempt to point out the line of duty for others in the matter. To do that with any chance of success, the whole question would require to be opened and discussed; yet I would

add, that, with the knowledge I have of the effects
and results of intoxicating liquors, on the mind
and body, the present and future happiness of
all concerned, *I could not, as a Christian, countenance the drinking habits of our day.*

But to the narrative. By the time I had gone
the round of my visitations to the parents, the
second session was nearly ended. I closed it by
a public examination, at which there was a good
turn out of ministers, teachers, parents, and
others interested in education. I had no wish
to make a vain show of my pupils, but I felt
proud of the manner in which they acquitted
themselves. They did their best, no doubt, but
they underwent no previous or set preparation,
as is generally the case. I had ever detested the
foolish plan, on such occasions, of burdening
children's memories with tasks to be repeated as
a parrot says "pretty Polly." We merely gave
a fair specimen of the week's round of studies,
now and then dwelling on such branches as any
of the audience might suggest. But while I
avoided much of the hypocritical and ruinous
practices at examinations, I was foolish enough
to adopt the old and often unjust mode of giving
prizes. I spent about thirty shillings on them,
and in their distribution, our harmony and
joy was marred. The greatest difficulty was
in giving the right prize to the right person.
In our highest class there were a boy and
a girl equal in knowledge and hardiness. The
minister who undertook the task of judging who
were the winners, gave the prize to the girl. I
did not object to this, but I proposed to give the
boy a book of the same kind. The scholars and
all present agreed to this, and yet the girl's father

was offended, and the minister has scarcely spoken to me since. This opened my eyes to the folly and injustice of humbug parading and unjust rewarding. I would have teachers consider this point more closely, and they will find, as a general rule, the poor and the timid suffer at set examinations. Both of these pupils were well-behaved; but the girl belonged to the middle-classes, while the boy was a poor orphan. She had plenty of time and opportunity to learn at home, he had little or none of either; yet in the class he was her equal!

Chapter VIII.

DURING my second vacation, I again visited Edinburgh; but not so much to see sights this time as to learn. I attended various classes during my stay, and an increased success attended my return to Dundee. My school filled at once, and I was now more at home among my obedient and affectionate *charge*. I was monarch of all I surveyed, and they were my willing subjects. I asked them if they would help me to govern without corporal punishment, and, of course, their ready answer was in the affirmative. We entered, on trial, for a week, and succeeded; then a month, and succeeded; and finding my way clear, I banished the *taws*.

This triumph induced me to make another trial. I found that as a rule children at church and the Sabbath-school were very restless, so I thought of watching to see where the blame lay. I began to deliver short addresses every Wednesday afternoon; and I succeeded in gaining the attention of the children by awakening their understandings. Many of their parents came to hear me, and they liked the addresses. At first, the topics were of a general nature, a change each time, on such subjects as the biography of some great and worthy person. Having trained them to the habit of listening and thinking, I opened and finished several courses of addresses, and with the same success. This experiment cost me no little time and thought; but it also improved my mind and heart; and suggested to me the propriety of having churches or meeting places on Sabbath *for children* where they would listen to *discourses prepared for them.* I am still convinced that were such places opened, and proper persons appointed, our youth would rise in the scale of knowledge and morals; and surely too much cannot be done for children.

I was glad of this success, and hence ventured again. Besides the ordinary branches taught in the school, I opened classes for botany, &c. That I might the more effectually carry out this undertaking, I wrote to a friend, Mr. George (now Professor) Lawson, asking the aid of his experience. From his kind and useful letter, I give this extract:—

"I highly approve of your proposal to teach your young charge the rudiments of natural history. It has long been my conviction that were the people of Britain more addicted to the study of such a pleasant subject, they would be all the happier for it. *It would greatly improve their moral feelings.*"

I carried out my plans with pleasure and profit to my pupils and to myself. Our botanical rambles were frequent and delightful. I shall merely give one instance illustrative of the fine feeling manifested by those who joined us in our search after flowers and plants. On a summer afternoon we were exploring a beautiful green bank, dotted with young and flourishing trees. A girl was before us, her eyes caught a sweet flower, and she exclaimed, "Oh! master, do come to see this lovely flower;" and the next moment she kissed it most affectionately. Not many minutes after, I was coming down the bank, and was just about to step upon a bonnie gowan, when another of my little band called out, "Oh! Sir, do spare the daisy, it is at your foot," and the tone was such as to let one know she spoke because she felt. I was glad. I remembered my friend Lawson's word, as to the refining tendency of natural history. I thought when such feeling and affection was bestowed on a flower, more would be given to a worm, and so on up to man and the Creator of all.

This, too, was a happy hit. By a succession of such efforts or experiments, I felt convinced that by firmness and affection, and the ability to lead and to teach, the rudest boy or girl might be trained to the love and practice of any good principle. But my anxiety and exertions were too much for my strength. By hard labour, in an over-crowded school, and close study, late and early, I was very much reduced, and had to close my third session a week or two before the usual time. I parted with my charge in the hope of meeting them again at the usual opening time; but the doctor told me I must give up teaching for a time, or take a small country-school. I went again to Edinburgh, not so much to learn as to get a change of air, and—shall I confess it?—to see "Aunty Maggie."

On my return to Dundee, still with the view of meeting my first and affectionate charge at Smithfield School, strangely enough, on my way up the Hilltown, I met a party from Kirriemuir who had come to ask my services for a school there. At first, and at once, I rejected the offer, because I could not think of parting with my pupils. But after the doctor's repeated injunctions, and the urgent advice of my friends, I consented to leave for a time. I visited the parents who sympathised with me, and they wished me better health and an early return.

At the general request, I sought out and placed another teacher in the school before I left. I also assembled the scholars, and remained with them and the new teacher for some days. Then came the farewell address, and the parting. Some of the elder pupils sobbed, endeavouring to restrain their emotion till they got home; others wept aloud; and not a few of the younger children hung on my coat, as if they could keep me by force. I cannot tell how I felt. The parting scene gave an additional proof of the love that existed between us as pupils and teacher.

CHAPTER IX.

ROUNDY-HILL School was the next scene of my labours. It is placed at the meeting points of the parishes of Airlie, Glammis, and Kirriemuir, each of which parishes paid a share of the salary. By many causes the school was reduced, and I at first feared lest my income would be greatly reduced; but pupils soon came from far and near, until I was drawing fees, the amount of which was equal to those of my former place. One reason of this unexpected success was the favourable impression produced by my testimonials upon the country people and the late Rev. Dr. Easton. Here is an extract from one of them—the Rev. Dr. M'Gavin's—he having the best opportunity of judging of my character and abilities:—

" Mr. James I. Hillocks has been intimately known to me for a considerable period as a zealous, efficient, and successful instructor of youth. His bearing towards the children is kindly, and his system of instruction very attractive and interesting to youth, and the progress of the pupils under his charge most creditable."

From him also I got my certificate of church membership, which I gave to the Rev. Mr. Stirling of the U. P. Church, Kirriemuir. In him I found an able minister and a kind friend. I was fortunate in getting comfortable lodgings and a worthy landlady. In short, I soon became a general favourite; and having gone there for the recovery of my health, I jaunted about till I became strong, hardy, and ruddy. I saw life in the country, plain and healthy, and I enjoyed it. not only got better and lively myself, but I had also the pleasure of being able to take my father out for a time, and of seeing him greatly improved before he left.

Though doated upon, comfortable, and successful, yet I was like a fish out of water, because I was away from my first charge. Knowing that they were experiencing a like feeling towards me, I wrote a letter to them, of which the following is the closing paragraph:—

" When I think of our past joys and our farewell—how you loved me so truly, and clung to me so closely, my heart fills.

So identified have been my life and feelings with yours, that even yet you are the subject of my daily thoughts and nightly dreams. Your presence was never annoying to me, and mine was always welcomed by you. On all our trials and triumphs we sympathized and rejoiced one with another. But, my dear young friends, we must not fret because of our separation. We can pray for each other, and God will still hear us. He is everywhere present, and will be with me here and you in Dundee. Nothing but distress could have taken me from you so early; and though we may not meet again as teacher and scholars, we may meet in heaven as the sons and daughters of our heavenly Father. Remember what good advices I have given you; respect your teacher, and obey your parents—that is the way to serve God. That He may bless and guide us and ours, is the earnest prayer of your former and affectionate teacher."

Up to the time of going to the country, I had, as a rule, wrought double work; and feeling now that I was well and strong, I could not bear the idea of being half idle. Being always well in advance of my pupils, and feeling that teaching was now to me an easy as well as a " delightful task," I again thought of making another effort to learn something more; and since Dr. Wood had favoured me with a little insight into chemistry, I had been anxious to know more of that science, and that of medicine. One day, Mr. Grant, chemist and druggist, Kirriemuir, entered into a conversation with me on the healing art and other topics. I told him of my desire to know more about them. He told me that if I would come to him he would do his best to impart what knowledge he had to me, and give me the advantage of what experience he had as a druggist. I accepted his offer; and we arranged that I should open the shop in the morning, and and remain there—doing a boy's drudgery, selling powders, &c.—till nine; to enter at five, and remain till ten in the evening, compounding and dispensing medicines—thus giving me between nine and ten to take breakfast and walk to my school—a distance of about two and a half miles—and from four till five to retrace my steps and take tea—the only time I had for reading and reflection being before seven in the morning and after ten in the evening. I continued to labour in this way for about a year and a half, at the end of which time I resigned the office of teacher, and devoted my whole time to the study and practice of medicine. Having finished my engagement with Mr. Grant, we parted on friendly terms. Here is an extract from his certificate:—

" James Inches Hillocks has been assisting me in my business as chemist and druggist, and I have had every reason to be satisfied with him as an honest, faithful, and diligent servant."

Having saved a pound-note or two, and finished my apprenticeship, I left for Edinburgh, and became a student at the Castlehill Normal Institution, at that time under the rectorship of the Rev. Mr. Davidson. But before I left I received testimonials from the ministers who visited my school at Roundy-Hill. I give an extract from one, as a specimen of the rest. I select the Rev. James C. Easton's, then of the South Church, and now of Old Meldrum, because he took a particular interest in the school, and was often there. He has also been very courteous and kind to me ever since—a good, hearty, country minister:—

" I can bear testimony to the merits of Mr. Hillocks, both as a Christian and an instructor; and I may mention that the ministers of the various denominations of the Christian Church in this neighbourhood have invariably testified their great satisfaction with his mode of teaching. He leaves his present situation from a natural desire to occupy a larger field of usefulness, and I trust he will not be long in securing such a place—to which he is so well entitled on account of his character, talents, and acquirements."

I went to this institution with the view of becoming a better teacher; but, to my astonishment, I saw very little in it I could call improvements. The teaching there was not of the stamp I looked for; perhaps I entertained rather an elevated idea of Normal Schools. I paid for board and education, and yet I gave more attention to private lessons without than to what I was likely to get within. The *making* of teachers, like the making of ministers and poets, is a very difficult task. All three must have the elements in themselves, but these may be cultivated; and a Normal School *should* help the man or woman whom Nature endows with the rare but requisite qualifications. Having been impressed with the idea that this institution was far behind the notions I had formed, by reading, of what Normal Schools and public teachers should be, and having learned, through the rector, that I could not get a situation out of it unless I left the U. P. Church, I bade adieu, convinced that a teacher, to be useful, must have more in him than what he gets at the Normal Institution.

From the time I began to feel the want of a school education, and felt that I could not very well understand the school-books on grammar, I had resolved, as soon as I was able, to write a small treatise on that and other subjects. I now thought I should make the attempt, and the " NEW WRITER " was the result. While under Mr. Davidson, I so far broke the rules as to buy a halfpenny candle, and write by its light in the dormitory after the gas was put out. What I wrote at night I revised in the morning when taking my walk in the Meadows. I saw the tractate through the press before I left, and was fortunate enough to meet with a good firm in that of Johnstone & Hunter, by whose efforts it has long since gone through the third edition. The design of this little manual is to assist those who have not had the benefit of a school education; and I was delighted to see it well received by the press and the public. A reviewer says:—

"In Mr. Hillock's little book we find outlines of English Grammar admirably laid down; indeed, in a way which leaves no doubt of the author being perfectly master of his subject, and of his being a gentleman in every way well-qualified for the discharge of his duties as a teacher of youth. The little treatise is not only adapted for schools, but can be studied with benefit by grown-up persons."

CHAPTER X.

FROM Edinburgh I went again to Dundee, where, before many weeks, I was surrounded by many of my former pupils. Some, indeed, had been removed, and some had fallen asleep in Jesus; but past associations were soon recalled, and sweet affections re-stirred. We were happy again as teacher and scholars, but only for one year. My class-room in six months became too small. We got another, double the size; and in six months more it, too, was not large enough to hold all who came.

·Finding my health again giving way under the hard labour, in a crowded school; and finding, too, that every church, but the one to which I belonged, was willing—if I would change—to help me, as a teacher, to reach the summit of my ambition, I resolved to adopt another mode of saving money to get the education and training requisite for the pulpit, by opening a shop and taking the advantage of my experience as a druggist. I had not much with which to start business, but I had a good turn for it, and was not long in succeeding beyond my expectation. There were two needing what help I could render. I took my sister home as housekeeper; and being requested to open a select class for advanced pupils, I took my father to wait in the shop during my absence, which was never more than an hour at a time. I was glad to see them more comfortable than they were. My sister got married, and I took to lodgings again; and finding what was considered a good opening—a larger shop, and nearer the centre of the town—I removed, and again did well. It was here where I enjoyed the pleasure of long and frequent visits from Mr. Campbell (previously mentioned), the author of "Campbell's Collection," and several other works. He was writing at the same time, and did me the honour of asking my advice on various occasions. Not only so, but he was also as ready as he was able to help me; for I had been, and was, trying the use of the pen. He, by mere accident, had seen some of my first attempts at verse: the lines already given, "My mammy's awa'," won his approbation, though, when he first saw them, they were roughly written, mechanically at least. This induced him to examine and correct my juvenile efforts. We selected forty pieces, which he suggested should be called "My Juvenile Wailings." To feel our way, and see if the public thought as he thought, he advised me to send one piece to the newspapers. I did so: it was afterwards printed on cards, and sung in schools and at concerts. This induced me the more readily to prepare the "Wailings" for the press; but they, along with the MSS. of "Notes of a visit to Edinburgh," "Tales for children," &c. (being in one MS. volume), were stolen from my counter when almost ready for the printer. This loss cost me some nights' sleep, but I grieved most for the verses.

One incident leads to another: the sending of "My mammy's awa'" to the *Arbroath Guide*, then under the able editorship of Mr. Kennedy, led to my acquaintance with that gentleman, and to the writing of the "Passages in the life of a young weaver," which first appeared in that newspaper. In writing to me anent these "Passages," he says:—

"I shall be very gratified by making the *Guide* the medium of your valuable lucubrations; for, from your experience of what you are to treat, valuable, I doubt not, they will be. Be assured that every attention will be paid to the contributions you may be pleased to favour me with."

The "Passages" were as successful as a pamphlet as they were in the newspaper: every copy has long since gone. The press was also favourable: only one newspaper of local standing came out against the little book, and that opposition did me good. There was another start-up rag which endeavoured to make a hit by abusing and trying, as was said, "to crush" the "young weaver." At that time Gilfillan was writing his "Bundle of Books" for *Hogg's Instructor*—a publication that should have lived, and would have paid, had it not given way to one of higher pretensions. Evidently from a generous motive, he therein reviewed my humble production, and spoke of it in a manner which made me call upon the critic, and thank him for his kind consideration in noticing the simple but genuine narrative. That was my first introduction to him; but many are the meetings we have had, and many are the kind and encouraging words he has said about me and to me since. It is curious how an ill *turn* becomes a good one. This is one of the mysteries of Providence, which proves the kindness of the All-Supreme.

Shortly after this little triumph in my second attempt at authorship, an important event followed. "Aunty Maggie" became somewhat ill, and left her place in Edinburgh, to be with her parents in Lochee for a time. I was a favourite with the old people, and called often *before she came*, but now they observed the later and earlier calls. They had a beautiful set of rose bushes in front of their neat cottage, and some hardy flowers in their garden, and I went, of course, for my morning and evening bouquet. Many handsome ones I got, all the sweeter that they were gathered by the hand I loved to clasp. Were I to tell "the reason why," some surly, burly bachelor would say, "All a hoax;" those of other notions know all about the secret; so I would merely mention that her beauty and worth made me break the resolution I had formed—not to marry till I should *finish* my education, as the phrase goes. But I have never had cause to regret having met Aunty Maggie; and I thank God she became mine, and that to this day she is as lovely, as loving, and as enduring as when I got the " faithful yes."

It is said, "When *poverty* comes in at the door, *love* goes out at the window." We do not believe that, though we have felt most of the ills that attend that *crime*—I say " crime," because those who are afflicted with it, whether honest or self-inflicted, are treated as criminals. Fervent, true, and deep-rooted holy affection never grows cold. There are ladies called lovely and graceful, whose personal charms and high politeness may arrest the attention and captivate the heart of him who looks for external beauty only: the woman with such attractions and the man with such fancies may become husband and wife, and may be happy, but there are ninety-nine chances to one against them. I do not mean by this to convey the idea that the beauteous maiden may not become a noble wife—that a faultless form and a generous deed are incompatible—that the perfection of human beauty is inconsistent with the highest moral sublimity. No; but, to act a noble part in the midst of poverty and distress— of agonies which are like to burst the heart, and tears which scorch the cheek, there must be more than a developed form and a graceful dignity. There must be purity as well as beauty, elevated piety as well as matured powers, or moral ruin is all but certain. It is the " unadorned beauty," imbued with meekness and piety, filled with confiding love and unwavering trust, that is the helpmate to bear one up while bowed down with the deadly weight of poverty or the sickening influence of distress. The affectionate fidelity, tender solicitude, the counsels, and prayers of a devoted wife, impart a new glory to all that is bright; while her deep yearnings, and the sobs of her unaffected mourning, even when she can scarcely do more than make the darkness visible, adds to her queenly womanhood and matronly dignity; and she becomes the more beautiful and endearing for her sadness, imparting a happiness which none but those who have come through a fiery furnace can know, or even imagine.

All we possessed of these qualities was soon to be tested. Even before our union, misfortune's blast began to tell what was coming. Except a few pounds, my business was clear and all my own; and I believed I could not only keep the object of my choice happy and comfortable, but that we would save something to enable me, as soon as possible, to go to Edinburgh College, for I had not yet lost sight of my chief aim. We agreed to open another druggist's shop at Broughty-Ferry, a bathing village four miles east of Dundee. As there was no such business there, the idea seemed to carry with it the appearance of prudence and benefit; but in less than three months from the time we fixed the day of our marriage, I had three considerable losses. The third was only a few days before that which "linked our destiny" to each other—the loss of my health, and nearly my life. I was injured and robbed at a dreary place on the road between Dundee and Lochee. Maggie was only the more anxious that the ceremony should be performed, that she might have the opportunity of waiting upon me. It was a blessing she was so firm and decided. None but an affectionate wife could have attended me so carefully and so kindly; and had I not been so nursed, I could not have survived.

Ailing as I was, we went to our new abode in Broughty-Ferry, and as soon as I got a little better I began to attend to the business, which increased every day for several months.

Both of us were well liked by the inhabitants. My helpmate, was of the same disposition as myself, and knowing how I had laboured before our marriage among the poor, and did my best to help them to help themselves, she encouraged me to begin the good work again. I had also delivered several lectures in Broughty on temperance and other social questions, so that the folks knew me somewhat, and not a few of those who liked to see the right advancing came about me. Our first effort was the re-organization of a Total Abstinence Society, which, when we left the place, was flourishing, and is still doing good; but, to our grief, and the sorrow of not a few, the means of usefulness and of living were taken from us all of a sudden, and that by intrigue. Having got our tidy shop well stored and prepared for the bathing season—the harvest of watering places—our hope increased with my health and success; but we lost our all, and some busy-bodies tried to rob us of our good name; yes, and even professed friends and professing Christians turned their backs and let their tongues loose upon us. We could not help mourning, but we had a clear conscience; and we knew that truth stands the severest test, and that justice would triumph, if not here, at least hereafter. As the case is still pending in the Court of Session, perhaps it would not be prudent to give a detailed account of the disaster. Writing to a friend, I took occasion thus to refer to the matter:—

"Even yet the agony and anguish of the past makes me shudder. Had I been the only sufferer the affair would have been bad enough; but, alas! my partner in life, poor creature! has also partaken of the sad calamities, and is still suffering from their direful effects. Words could not describe the dark shades of grief and sadness caused by our sudden translation from comparative success to positive adversity. During the first six months of our married life the benignant smile of affection, the subdued tone of fear, the eager brightness of hope, the sympathetic look of compassion, and the suppliant expression of devotion, alternately bespoke the state of our feelings and affections; and oh, dear Laing! these did not only partake of a deeper hue during the next six months, but to them were added the dejection of despair and the excitement of frenzy. The brutal assault of midnight robbers drove us on to the verge of the grave, and the malicious doings of noonday plunderers pitched us into the vortex of poverty. You will see by the enclosed copy of the summons that the villanous project, biased judgment, and illegal proceedings against me, are to be tried at a higher court. Whatever may be said about my appealing to the Court of Session, I know that my aim is vindication, and, if possible, reparation. I sue not for private vengeance. Wealth and influence may protect the merciless pillagers and their rogueish accomplices, and thereby stem the channel of justice; but if the law does not rescue the value of my property, it may maintain my character as irreproachable. But, as you know, though the administration—which is, or should be, the aim and end of law—restore to me my means and the comfort which they could afford, yet no compensation can ever repay the injury to me and mine—money cannot heal wounded feelings."

CHAPTER XI.

AFTER this wholesale ruin I became very ill again, and so did my partner. Imagine our sorrowful condition, sick and penniless, not able to work, with but few to sympathize with us. There was one who knew our sorrow and felt with us, as a young but thoughtful girl could: this was the "Aggie" who was the means of my first introduction to her aunt—one of my first pupils, and now our dear niece. She lived with us during the first year of our marriage, and her company was pleasant. She has a place in our affections only second to our own beloved children.

I had been writing "Sophia," and as soon as I could attend on her passage through the press, she was introduced to society. But I was too poor to bring her successfully forward. Gilfillan, referring to her, says:—

"She is not gaudily dressed, or expensively adorned, but she is *simplex munditiis*. Her virtue is unquestionable, and so is her good temper and taste; now and then she moves gracefully, and certainly all her steps are tuned to the music of high morality and genuine religion."

And yet this creature did not suit the purpose for which she was created, neither in point of general benefit nor private gain. "A glance at society" was the aim, but, as I have said, I was too poor.

Again my life was in danger, the doctor prescribing the country air as the only chance of surviving. How was this to be had? The inventive faculties of a loving wife help greatly in times of distress and difficulty. Frail as Maggie was, she, by her own hands, earned the means that let me away to Kirriemuir among my old friends, who were as kind as ever. We parted with little or no hope of meeting again on earth; but the means were blessed. From Roundy-Hill I got to Blairgowrie, where I experienced a still greater change for the better. Letters now supplied the place of conversations; and many were the kind and moving notes I received from her.

As soon as I was able, I came home to Broughty-Ferry; and some time after I was offered the situation of teacher of a small school under the patronage and support of Sir James Ramsay, Bart., Bamff, near Alyth. We were glad of a home, and were soon in our new abode. If the income was not large, the labour was not hard.

The people were very kind, and those who were able never paid the fee without giving something in addition. Sir James, too, was very generous and attentive, personally and through his housekeeper, Mrs. Brunton, a worthy and sensible, friendly, and *couthy* woman.

On the morning of the 13th November, 1852, we were gladdened by the gift of a lovely boy. We had read much about the first baby, but now we realized the inexpressible feeling. What a sensation crept over me when I first looked into his sweet wee face. About him I wrote verses by the yard, and letters by the score. His mother, poor creature, was long very ill; her past fatigue and sore grief told now upon her. It was my turn to become nurse, and I was astonished at my strength during her illness. The boy was named George Gilfillan.

An express message came from my father; we went to see him; he was lying on his death-bed. We were overcome when we saw him, but he told us he was happy. All that he wished was to be saved from a pauper's coffin, and that he might be carried to the grave cleanly and tidy. We had not much, but we were able to gratify his wish. "I am ready; I have gotten all I wished for—I wait God's time," he said, and kissed and blessed our little boy, and wished us continued happiness. He died in a few days afterwards, and I was thankful I was able to perform a son's part to an ill-used and sadly neglected father. I thought of his words to me when he did his best to give me a few weeks' schooling; I thought, too, how those who fight our battles and win our victories are treated—robbed of their health and the best of their days, and left to starve—to die in poverty.

A correspondence was opened between the Rev. Mr. Leckie, of Muirton U. P. Church, and myself, anent the school there. We entered into an engagement, and I went there, believing I was now able for a larger class than I had, and that I might thereby increase my income. I took with me testimonials from Sir James and the parish minister. Here is an extract from Sir James':—

"I have every reason to be satisfied with Mr. Hillocks. He appears to me to be an able and a successful teacher; and I may add, that the minister of the parish, to whom he is well known, and the other ministers who have attended examinations of the school when under his charge, entertain a high opinion of his qualifications, and of his general character."

I had the pleasure of reading a paragraph in the *Dundee Advertiser* recounting, in pleasant terms, the various efforts I had made for the general and educational good.

When we arrived at the Mary-Kirk station, one of the committee was waiting to lead us to our new home. He, to my surprise, said I had been there before. I could not credit that; but as we approached I found he was correct. It was no other than Luthermuir I was nearing—the place where I landed some years before—the poor wanderer in search of work. My old friends came laughing round me to bid me welcome, this time as their teacher.

Mr. Leckie addressed his letters, "Muirton" (the name of the spot upon which the church was), "Laurencekirk" (the post-town at that time for Luthermuir). It was as well: had I known where I was going, I would not have undertaken the duties, such were my impressions of the place when there as a weaver. But here I was; back I could not go: I prepared myself for the work.

There was room; but I knew the hearts and hearths of the people; so I prayed God to help me, and He heard my prayer. I was not strong, but I was willing, and I had a helping hand, as well as a good heart, in Maggie. To particularize the varied duties I had to perform, from the time I went till the time I left Luthermuir, would require more space and time than I have at my command; I shall merely give the valedictory address. As I feel proud and thankful for it, because of the kindly spirit which it breathes, I give it in full:—

"DEAR MR. HILLOCKS,—In the name of the friends of reform here, we hail with delight the present opportunity of expressing our high estimation of your excellent worth. Fourteen months ago, when you was providentially placed amongst us, we were glad to hear of your character, zeal, and abilities, as a man, a Christian, a teacher, a lecturer, and friend of humanity. Then we expected your invaluable assistance in the work of domestic and social reform; and now we rejoice that your eminent devotion, deep earnestness, and unwearied activity, have been so applied that the beneficial results have far outreached our most sanguine expectation.

"We need not particularize the varied offices you have so energetically fulfilled since you came here. All who have witnessed the zealous manner in which you have performed your arduous and philanthropic duties must be aware that your great efforts have been worthy of your generous heart. The manifest good which has been effected by your mental exertions has been graciously blessed by our Heavenly Father, and now stirs a deep sense of gratitude and lasting affection in us towards you.

"As a teacher, your merits are well known here and elsewhere, as is amply attested by numerous testimonials from able judges, but also by the rapid progress of the pupils under your charge.

"And while we congratulate you as an able and conscientious instructor of youth, we also rejoice that your field of labour has not been confined to the school-room. You have, with tongue and pen, come boldly out against the evils of our day, especially that of intemperance. Before you came, there was little resistance offered to this giant evil here; but now it is met, and, in some measure, conquered. Then there were but a few who acknowledged and practised the principles of abstinence societies, of strict temperance; but now, by your individual exertion, we have a large and flourishing society based on these principles—a society which, by the blessing of God, has already done much good, and caused many of its members to bless its existence.

"But besides the private and public advocacy of temperance, you have also opened the other avenues to the people's respect and affection. Not the least of these is the Christian manner in which you have successfully endeavoured to cheer the drooping heart and enlighten the darkened soul. This you have done, not only publicly as a teacher and lecturer, but also privately as a missionary. You have also been of eminent service to the sick as an administrator of medicines; many have shared the benefit of your advice in the repelling of those disorders incidental to the human frame.

"And now, dear sir, though we must part, and mourn your loss, yet we are grateful to God, and thank you for the time we have had your services. You leave with our best wishes for comfort and happiness towards yourself and family wherever you go. May God be with you to protect you from danger, and guide you in all your efforts to promote the cause of temperance and humanity. Go, then, dear sir, apply yourself with all your heart and energy in the mental and moral emancipation of the masses as you have done here and elsewhere. May a wide field of usefulness soon give full scope to your talents. Wherever Providence may cast your lot, remember this place in your prayers; and be assured that you carry with you the warmest affection of many a heart.

"Accept of this address, as the earnest though faint expression of our gratitude.

(Signed) "DAVID DONALD, President.
"JOHN S. WILSON, Secretary, *pro tem.*

"Luthermuir, February 3, 1855."

With this address I received a tangible token of respect from the friends of social and moral reform. The *Montrose Review*, in noticing my leaving, justly characterized the meeting as "numerous and highly respectable." The parting was a touching scene; all were filled with emotion. I have visited the place since, and found the hearts as warm as ever.

CHAPTER XII.

WE made for Dundee once more. Home is the centre of attraction. By the time we paid our fares and luggage charges thither we were in possession of 20s.—exactly the same sum which I had when I arrived at Lochee from Luthermuir, years before. Feeling much improved in health, I thought I would now try the town life again, but did not know what to put my hand to. I was advised by my friends to try my old business of druggist and stationer, and I got a shop at the west-end, Perth Road. When about to close with the landlord, he said, " We are strangers to each other, and it is natural that I should ask security for the rent." " Natural enough," I replied; " but were any person in my position to ask me to be surety for him I would not consent; and I would not ask a man to do for me what I could not do for him." He admitted the force and honesty of what I said, and only asked a reference. In a moment I gave a number of names with whom I had done business in Dundee. On my calling again, he put the keys in my hand, saying that my character would get a dozen of shops.

I was glad of one; and what to put in it was the next question. Its construction was such that we made a dwelling-house of it as well as a shop, and this was a saving and a filling-up at the same time. When we got in we had only 2s. 6d. in the world to begin business and keep house with; but I got a few stationery things on sale from one person, and a little credit from another, and some bottles and medicines from a third on a few weeks' credit; and it so happened that the person who had preceded me in the shop had left the counter, shelving, and gas-fittings; so that I had just to arrange my small stock and open the door. By the time this was done, we were reduced to one halfpenny. For days and weeks the people did little else than look at our scanty array; and how we made out to live it is hard to say: it was not on ham-an'-egg anyhow.

As strange things will be, in the midst of this difficulty, home came a bonnie lassie. After all, we did not regret this; the wee thing was looked upon as a sweet gift rather than a burden: we would not have given her away again for all the wealth of Britain. This gave us an "Aggie" of our own, and made a lovely pair, and, as folks would flatteringly say, two miniature pictures of ourselves, real photographs, having excellent half-tones, shading off into a rich beauty.

After all, we made out, and had our quarter's rent ready by the time appointed, save 10s., which we borrowed for a week. We found our land-lord friendly, kindly, and accommodating.

As soon as the mother was able, she attended to house affairs, and, during my absence, to the shop. We saw that though the business might ultimately pay well, and keep us comfortable, if we had the stock to put in it and the cash to make a display—for drug-shops, like public-houses, need some glitter to make them attractive—so we thought of adding to our income by doubling our labour. I opened a school at the West Port. This was hard for both of us; but what will two who work hand to hand not do to stand upright and honourable. We were tired in the evening, but we were happy, and the morning brought us refreshment, and made us ready to renew our exertions.

Being what was considered established, and being known in the west-end, as well as throughout the town, as anxious to do a little good without as well as within, I was often asked to address meetings on various subjects in connection with the temperance and other good movements. For the Dundee Band of Hope—then under the active management of my friend, James Scrymgeour—I composed and delivered my three lectures on "Mrs. Hemans as a *daughter*, a *mother*, and a *poet*."

Before I close this sketch I shall mention an incident which occurred during these labours of love. One reason why the people of the Perth Road gathered round me in my efforts to be useful, was because I was near the spot where I spent a portion of my childhood and boyhood, not many yards distant from the school in which I was taught the A B C, and only a few more paces from the houses where I sat at the pirn-wheel. My father at that time weaved and I *winded* in one of the middle shops in Beattie's Square, Taylor's Lane; but now the place had been taken for a mission-station, a Sabbath-school, and a meeting-place. It so happened that the desk and the chairman's place were on the spot where my father's loom was wont to be; and one night, when giving a lecture there, I found myself speaking on the very spot where I, a few years before, had driven the wheel. When thinking of this the sensation I felt was such that, for the moment, I stopped short and related the circumstance, which drew from the audience a hearty round of applause. This was regarded by them as a triumph, and I felt something like the same feeling: it elevated my desires and hopes; and I once more wished I might yet possess some of this world's means and influence, not only to be able to keep my fireside comfortable, but to be enabled to make more and greater advances by way of improving myself and others, of doing my duty, and forwarding the happiness of man. When there as the pirner, I was the aspiring boy—as the lecturer, I was the aspiring man.

I must now close, not for want of matter, but because the time is up (May 14th, 1856). Whether or not I may obtain a prize, I shall be no worse for the effort; it has recalled the past to my memory, and wherein I have erred I will be on my guard in future; and in so far as I have succeeded, so much has the desire increased to become still more useful.

Chapter XIII.

LIMITED space forbids my extending the continuation of the autobiography as I otherwise would have done; and I shall therefore only glance at a few of the leading incidents.

The income derived from my school was a help for a time. My pupils increased; and I laboured so hard in an over-crowded class-room that my health again failed, and inflammation laid me aside. Though I was long very weak, I rallied, thanks to the care and skill of my friend, Dr. Lothian, who, to the grief of many, has since been suddenly cut off by typhus fever, in the midst of a deserving popularity, and an increasing usefulness. I removed my classes to a district nearer home. Though my new class-room was larger, many of my pupils followed me from the centre of the town. It was soon as crowded as ever, and every day I was growing paler and thinner. My helpmate, too, was suffering from close confinement. Some one of the professions had to be given up, and I resigned the more congenial — the teaching. To please my pupils, and help, as they thought, to make up for their disappointment, I closed my school by a public examination. When I saw how my pupils acquitted themselves, heard how parents and others were delighted, I felt that teaching was my work, and almost regretted having resolved on giving it up; but I had learned, as many others have, that it is slow murder — even if one had the chance — to obtain a respectable income from a common, independent public school. A teacher belonging to the United Presbyterian Church, as I did and still do, has not a fair chance of success. Those belonging to the Free and Established are supported by salaries and influence, and can therefore afford to lower their fees. I mention this, not by way of complaint, but simply as a reason why, dearly as I loved, and still love, teaching, I sought other means by which to support my family.

But what made me carry out this resolution, perhaps, earlier than I would have done, was an offer made me by the proprietor of the *Weekly Express*, a Dundee newspaper. We entered into an engagement, which I soon found to be a mistake. After labouring hard for several months, I resigned; and, to punish me for doing so, I was denied my wages. Shortly after I left, the

Express ceased to exist, and the trustee offered me threepence in the pound.

But I might have made up for this mishap, had not long and severe domestic affliction followed. Now it became my turn to serve in the shop and to nurse. The bairnies, as well as myself, learned how dreary and sad the house is when "the mither is sick."

After she recovered, I made some use of my pen. I composed a lecture on "Wallace; lessons from his life and times." This I delivered, by invitation, to a flourishing society of intelligent young men. It was well received by the audience, and favourably noticed by the press.

I received a letter from Leith, written by Mr. Ness, a true-hearted enthusiast, in behalf of a committee who wished my lecture delivered there, with the view, as I afterwards learned, of stirring the popular mind in favour of the Wallace Monument. I went; the audience was large and respectable, and the committee paid me honourably.

This visit suggested the idea of trying to push my fortune in Edinburgh. I informed my friend Gilfillan of my intention, who, with his usual readiness to aid those who need his help, gave me some notes of introduction. Here is an extract from one of them :—

"He has bravely and manfully struggled on—now, with great acceptance, instructing youth—and now labouring with no little energy and perseverance in the literary vineyard. He has, more recently, had some experience in the management of a newspaper, and in that capacity has shown very considerable taste, tact, and discretion. I have no doubt he will, as he deserves, yet rise in the newspaper press, and give satisfaction to any who may employ him. His habits are industrious, and his character irreproachable."

Chapter XIV.

I FOUND, when once out, it was difficult to get in. For once fear began to master hope. Night after night I paced the floor of my lodgings in distraction. Letters of disappointment one after another came in. I would have gone back to Dundee, but trade, generally, was dull, and our business was thereby suffering. Being introduced to Mr. Mathers, he secured my services in connection with his *Scottish Time Table;* but that was only for a few days at the end of each month. While enduring the misfortunes of one out of a place, I asked myself the question, Might I not use what abilities I had been favoured with, for payment, now that I was not in a position to apply them merely for love? I had before me a bundle of papers, containing such sentences as this:—" Mr. Hillocks is a consistent abstainer of many years' standing ; an earnest, effective, and eloquent advocate of total abstinence; one who has done good service to the cause by his tongue and pen."

This reminded me of my past efforts, and led me to think that if I had a claim on any body of men, it was on those composing the Temperance Movement. Accordingly I applied, but there was no opening—no chance for me. What a difference, thought I. Not long before this, I could not have supplied the demand made upon me for addresses, though I had been divided into half-a-dozen speakers; but now some of my Leith friends suggested that I should deliver a lecture there on our national bard, he, at that time, being the hero of the day. I set to work, and in a fortnight I was prepared with my lecture on "Burns, as a Poet and a Teacher, considered in relation to the errors of his time, and those of our day." With high expectation, I went to Leith on the night appointed, but soon the damper was placed upon my hopes. A rival lecturer was in the field. I was to speak on Monday, he on Tuesday, on the same branch of the same subject. I was told that his announcement and mine were almost word for word; and my placards being first out, were nearly all covered by his. I was aided only by a few, he was under the auspices of a society. I received a letter from one of the committee, stating that what was done was not "intended opposition." My audience, though not so large as it otherwise would have been, was respectable, and the lecture was favourably noticed by the *Witness*, and other papers.

Immediately on the back of this, another affair happened of the same nature in some points, but withal more disastrous to me. Unjust, uncalled for, and I may add, cruel as it was, I could suppose the actor would not have had the heart to play such a part, had he for a moment thought of the possible results. I verily believe it was that deed which deprived me of the few pounds that would have broken up and cleared away the darkening clouds that were surrounding me. It is fearful sport to snatch from a sinking man the last means of saving himself.

I now wrote several parties who were due me various sums, but only a few answered my gentle notes, and those who did, made "inability" their excuse. Nor was there wanting at that time an invitation to a meeting of creditors, to see if I would be content with part at a given date.

My helpmeet was also uneasy in Dundee. She struggled hard, but had to give way. On the Saturday, she wrote requesting that I would be at the station on the arrival of the first train from Dundee, as I should then find a parcel for me. I went, but scarcely had the train stopped when I heard the dear voices calling "Papa! Papa!" Most heartily did I welcome her as the heroine of my heart, worthy of a better fate than had been hers since she became mine. Now burst forth the thunderstorm which a few weeks' salary would have averted, but which no effort of ours, more than we had made, could have prevented. Then gathered the gossips, and oh! how they enjoyed the pouring of their viperous slander into our wounded and bleeding hearts! Often have we been sinned against, especially by tippling gossips, but never more so than on this occasion. To have believed them, the public would have thought we were due one half the world to the other half. Their story was a parody on the story of "Three black crows." But while this was the base conduct of the dogs and their doggerel companions, the sober, the honest, and the respectable felt for us, and maintained our honesty of purpose. Those to whom we were due anything knew that it was neither idleness nor misspending that caused our misfortune, and that their money would be forthcoming as soon as we got it. Had we obtained our own, we could have paid all twice over.

Here we were, in Edinburgh lodgings, and I may say almost without an income. What could I do? Anxiously did I hope, and sorely did I strive to find some way to bring my family honourably to Edinburgh, and to keep them respectably and comfortably; but now I had to go to Dundee to make arrangements regarding the shop articles and other things. Every thing had to go, not for what it was worth, but for what it would bring.

There was yet one thread of hope. The Law Agent, who had the Broughty-Ferry case in hands, had told me he was to bring it to a close, and from the proof I had, and still have in my possession, against the parties in the action, I felt convinced the day was mine, and that having obtained my own, I could settle with all and have something to myself. But still the case stands as it was.

When almost in despair, my friends, Johnstone and Hunter, proved their friendship by employing me in connection with their truly popular and really useful publication, *The Christian Treasury*. They paid me honourably, and I did my best for their interest.

A blessing attended on the income thus derived. The term time came, and we reluctantly entered the premises I had previously taken in East Richmond Street. By this time we were enabled to get some things for the shop. We got on so well in a small way (my helpmeet, as before, taking the responsibility and labour in my absence), that I began to think the idea of going to college would soon be realized. Again I was asked to give lectures and addresses at soirees and other meetings. Yea, it came to this, that a society offered me something for a course of four popular lectures, on "Home, its Ties and Duties." On this course I bestowed no small attention.

The truth is, I wrought rather hard, and sat too closely. On the night on which I delivered the last, I felt very ill; and on the next morning symptoms of typhus fever were telling upon my exhausted frame. Another day and I had to yield; a few more, and I knew not where I was, nor what was doing.

CHAPTER XV.

MY heart and pen would alike fail me were I to attempt to describe the suffering, the sorrow, the poverty, and the hardships that followed; yet God was with us the while. A doctor was needed; we knew not one; yet he came in time. While we were perplexed, a carriage drove up to a passage opposite; it was Doctor Menzies. He did not need any pleading to come in: he at once told what was the matter. Another test of the strength, the affection, and devotion of my helpmeet! In her, God had not only given me an affectionate and endearing wife, but also a careful and skilful nurse—strong in that faith which soothes us in sorrow and fortifies us for the battle of life. Severe and dangerous as the fever was, still she had hope. Long did she watch me night and day. At last the good doctor's fine countenance brightened; I had crossed the roughest waters, near to the rude billows of Jordan's proud swelling; and now she felt the effects of her anxiety and fatigue.

On the Fast-day I was so far recovered that I could for a short time listen to what had happened, and even speak for a short period with our children. Poor dear creatures!—how the sweet smiles of joy shone through their bright tears of gratitude! Two offers had come—one of an editorship; and the other to become teacher at an institution; but my chances of recovery being so few, my friends could not wait; yet we regretted not, trusting in the future.

We were glad and grateful to God and the doctor, and even our children that night went to bed with lighter hearts than they had for some time; but this was another " hicht afore a howe." While we were absorbed, some one was watching an opportunity—our purse and all we had, save threepence, was stolen that day, and missed that night. Being now able to discern a little, I saw something was wrong, and asked what it was. The sad intelligence operated upon me so greatly that the doctor saw at once a change for the worse. He had to be told the cause—the whole truth. To the honour of his generous heart, he related the case to a willing friend, who, through him, sent 10s. more than once.

When I again got a little round, I would often, with bleeding heart, watch my poor nurse's motions, now so weak and pained that she could only *hirple* to and from my bedside by leaning on the chair or table near her. One morning the tea-canister, the bread-plate, and the meal-basin were empty; but God, through a benevolent lady, sent our breakfast, and many a meal besides. We felt the gratitude that bounds from the hearts of the honest poor. Long did I sit in the bed before I could be lifted to the fireside, and often did I sicken there. A couch was erected, that I might half lie and half sit.

F

This was an improvement; but then the wind would sweep about me, and sometimes the snow would drift through the holes of the sham partition which divided what was called a room from the shop; and this in a place which the landlord, by missive, was bound to make " habitable," and for which I was bound by the same to pay £20 yearly !

We had the offer of a place in Potter-row, and thinking any one would be better than what we had, we went to it without seeing it before hand. This was a pity. The walls were a mass of rotten clay, and living vermin. I have actually seen the hailstones dancing on the rotten floor. At night the candle would not burn because of the wind sweeping from hole to hole, and scarcely a day passed, in which we were not smoked like red herrings. But this much must be said for the hovel—it was a palace compared with many an attic and cellar called houses in Edinburgh, in which poor wretches are being murdered every day. This much I must say for the landlord, when he offered us the place, he said it was not fit for us, but we were welcome to whatever shelter it might afford; and really it was better than the hill-side, and not much worse than the Richmond Street shamble we left. And though the rent was at the rate of £3 3s., when I went to pay for the time I had of it, he told me he never intended to take rent for it from me.

But our Potter-row abode has its reminiscences. There we passed the first day of 1860, on the morning of which we had only three farthings in the world; and everything we could spare, and more, either sold or pledged; but we were sore and sick, and our stomachs did not crave much food. We felt for our children.

The morning of the ninth day after brought home a little stranger—as bonnie a wee lassie as ever saw the light of day. Now we had four gems, the brighter, the lovelier, the better their mother never saw—so valuable, that all the gold in the world could not buy any one of them. Why, we were never so rich. This event was the means of showing that indigence and kind-heartedness were not incompatible. Our neighbours did their best to help us.

Again, and unexpected as before, another letter came from the same lady, and in this, too, was a P.O. order for a pound-note. Though we have had many hard-up days, and been glad of anything to ward off the keen pangs of hunger, we have never wanted a whole day since. In gratitude we called our young stranger by the name of the kind lady.

Shortly after this I was introduced to some ladies, who asked me to help them as a mission teacher—to teach the rudiments of English, to impart sound principles, and to visit the parents. For this I was to receive three shillings weekly; but the lady, a good hearted and really sensible woman, who paid me, gave a shilling, and sometimes two more, and was very kind besides.

Another lady, young, amiable, and generous, visited us once or twice. We shall never forget her favours. She felt for us as one real Christian feels for another.

During the time I was laid up, my " Thoughts in Rhyme" had been standing in the press; but now I got it out, and, happily for me, it soon enabled me to clear all expenses connected with it, and also bring in a shilling now and then to help to keep the bones green. I feel proud of the critical notices concerning it; but I feel convinced that Gilfillan's "Introductory Sketch" was the greater source of attraction. The "Sketch," as has been well and frequently observed, is written "in a fine spirit of sympathetic and kindly appreciation." One extract will show how the narrative portion is written :—

"'He that winneth souls is wise,' says a great authority, and we venture to parody the expression thus—'He that winneth children must himself be a child,' partaking of many of the finer qualities which make childhood a thing so wonderful, so unique, and almost so divine. It is easy to terrify children —not difficult to cram them with knowledge—but to win them at once to yourself, and to the love of learning, is a rare and peculiar, although a simple seeming gift. It was to us, at least, always truly delightful to see our 'Young Weaver' presiding in what was sometimes called 'The Laddie's School'—a child amongst children—leading them, even as Una led by a line her milk-white lamb, by the unseen cord of love, to the green pastures and the still waters of knowledge, and by those ways of spiritual wisdom which are pleasantness and peace. In November, 1851, we had the pleasure of linking Mr. Hillocks' destiny to that of his excellent wife, who still continues to be his affectionate and attentive helpmeet, 'both of them,' he says, 'continuing to bless the day that made them one.' Our friend has diversified his teaching tasks by various literary productions. In these he has had to contend with many disadvantages, springing from his early want of thorough culture, but that he has issued so many books on such various subjects is highly creditable alike to his industry and abilities. His 'New Writer,' when it appeared, was very much commended by the press, as an useful and unassuming production. His 'Passages from the Life of a Young Weaver' is an exceedingly interesting little book—a record of his own experiences in early life—and has gone through several editions. His 'Viola,' 'Sophia,' &c., are earnest efforts to elucidate the social questions of the day, and display very considerable faculties of thinking, observing, and writing. And his Poems, now published, partake of much of that naivete, sweet simplicity and child-heartedness which we have attributed to his teaching. Mr. Hillocks was sometime connected with a Dundee newspaper, but left it owing to the scurrilous character which, in spite of his remonstrances, it attained. His own writings are all distinguished by a pure and high tone of morality, and his opinions on religious subjects are those of a liberal, but thoroughly orthodox, Christian."

Chapter XVI.

THIS little volume was also the means of introducing me to many whose names are respected, and whose friendship I now share and value. Till then, except my dear friend and minister, Mr. Thomas Knox, the earnest and talented philanthropist, was the first to find us out in our distress. I shall never forget the expression he used when he entered our hovel. The next who made me feel I was not forgotten was the Rev. Dr. Guthrie, and that by an invitation to breakfast. The party was large and lively, and the Doctor's fund of witty, humorous, and telling anecdote was as exhaustless as his knowledge of men and manners. I may here take the liberty to record one of them. It was told to illustrate the truth that those who expose error, and are called "fault-finders," and other harsh names, are not themselves without heart, are not always contaminated with the atmosphere in which they see it to be their duty to live and work.

"One Sabbath afternoon, in winter," said the Doctor, "Thackeray was going down the Canongate, Edinburgh, when his attention was called to three almost naked children, at a close end —their feet red as *collips*, yet singing

'There is a happy land,
Far, far away.'

This scene opened the floodgates of the fearless author's tender heart."

Before I left, the Doctor gave me an introductory note to Mr. Troup, then succeeding Mr.

Bayne to the Editorship of the *Witness;* nor was this his only effort in my behalf. It was only the other day I had the opportunity and pleasure of reading a letter he sent to a party respecting me. It was written in the Doctor's own style, and spoke of me in such a manner as led to the hope that better days are waiting me and mine.

Among the letters that came, all of which were more or less interesting, was one from an esteemed friend in London, offering me a responsible place on a newspaper there. But dearly as I loved the friend who wished me with him, and anxious as I was to work again, for the sake of my family, yet such was my weak state, and such were other circumstances, that I had to decline the London offer. I regretted this afterwards, and so did some of my friends; and yet, though I know what has happened here, I do not know what might have taken place there.

By the kind and united efforts of the young lady referred to, and the one who introduced us to her, a room was obtained for us, and we left the Potter-row ruins. How glad and grateful we were to be again in a place having the appearance of a house!

I continued to act as mission-teacher, and having formed new classes, I had a slight increase of pay. If I had had anything like an income, I could not have wished more congenial employment.

We soon found that though we had left the " ruins," their effects on our systems had not left us. Our children were drooping and ailing before we removed to our new abode; but now they became so ill that we began to ask, What, if now any of our darlings be taken from us ? The

youngest girl was the liveliest; but the rest—
particularly the boy, poor lad!—ran a hundred
chances to one for his life. Affliction knits closer
the cords of affection. Man's extremity is God's
opportunity. One day the doctor left a prescrip-
tion, but we had not a penny with which to get
it. A friend had written a pamphlet, worthy of
his head and heart. He gave me a few copies:
I sold three one forenoon, and this enabled us to
get leeches for our boy, which were, no doubt,
the means of saving his life.

Once more things began to brighten a little.
My friend, the Secretary for the Edinburgh City
Mission, kindly employed me for an hour or two
daily in his office, during the time work was pressing hard upon him. He is still a kind friend.

About this time another thoughtful friend
spoke a kind word for me to the Secretary
for the Soldiers' Friend Society, who, in a very
courteous letter, asked me to forward an application for a scripture-readership, and to enclose
what testimonials I had, that he might send
them on to London. I lost not a moment in
complying with his request; and most anxiously
did I wait the decision of the London Board,
which was all I could look for. The matter is
not yet settled; but should my application do no
more, it has been the means of gaining for me
the friendship of the Rev. Mr. Hall. A heartier,
kindlier gentleman I never met with—full of life
and love. And, as if to brighten my prospects,
I was, at this time, introduced to Professor
Blackie, who, as a mark of respect, and to help
me the better to gain my object, kindly offered
me a present of a ticket entitling me to all the
advantages of his Greek classes. I need not

say I was thankful.   The conversation was not long, but I felt, before we parted, that the scholar knew human nature as well as Greek.

———

READER,—For the present we part.   I trust you do not regret having gone thus far with me. It is not the life of an old man you have read, it is simply the sad story of one who has not yet passed the prime of life—of one who is anxious as ever to be useful—of one who, though he has not yet reached the "Far up height," is yet willing to climb the steep, yet determined as ever to rally round

> "The banner with the strange device,
> Excelsior !"

—of one who is yet waiting for work.   May God, through good friends, send it soon!

55 ROSEMOUNT BUILDINGS,
EDINBURGH, September 20, 1860.

PRINTED BY ROBERT RAE, 14 MAXWELL STREET, GLASGOW.